The World's Worst Networker: Lessons Learned By The Best From The Absolute Worst!

Timothy M. Houston

www.worldsworstnetworker.com

The World's Worst Networker:
Lessons Learned By The Best From The Absolute Worst

This publication is designed to provide accurate and authoritative information in regard to the subject matter covered. It is sold with the understanding that the publisher is not engaged in rendering legal, accounting, or other professional services. If legal advice or other expert assistance is required, the services of a competent professional should be sought.
>   –   From a Declaration of Principles jointly adopted by a
>   Committee of The American Bar Association and
>   a Committee of Publishers and Associations.

Edited by: Michael Amalfitano, MSW

Cover design and interior layout/design by

Holly Joffrion
Joffrion Designs

ISBN-13: 978-1453866801
ISBN-10: 1453866809

To Mom and Grandma Jean:

Two of the greatest networkers in the world.

Acknowledgments

This book was truly a labor of love and involved many people's thoughts, ideas and inspirations. There were times when I doubted that it would ever come to be, but with the support and encouragement of so many people it finally happened and I enjoyed every minute of it.

First a heartfelt "thank you" to each and every one of the contributing authors. Your willingness and embracement of the theme of this book exemplify why you are **THE BEST** networkers and the best people in the world. Without you, it would not have happened.

A very special thanks to Dr. Ivan Misner whose generosity provided the mentoring, encouragement, written resources and introductions that helped this book to manifest. I am forever grateful.

To my editor, Michael Amalfitano, MSW: thank you for capturing my writing style and voice better than anyone else.

Thanks to my Creative Director, Tim Seitz. Your genius never ceases to amaze me.

Very special thanks to my great friend and assistant, Ivan Radujko. Whenever I need you, you are there, ready to take on whatever challenges come your way.

Many thanks to my family and friends who are always wondering "what will Tim do next?" and are always supportive in my endeavors, no matter what they are.

To my wonderful partner, Richard: Thank you for your patience, your unending support and love. Without question, this project couldn't have happened without you.

About This Book

WARNING: This is not the typical "how-to network" book. In fact, it's more of a "how-not-to-network" program. What you are about to read is a collection of uncensored stories and experiences that occurred while networking, by me and by others from all over the world. Some are downright shocking and scary, while others are absolutely hilarious.

Some of the contributors to this project are well-known experts, trainers and best-selling authors on the subject of business networking. Others are everyday business people whose names, while they may not be immediately recognizable to some, are among the most productive, proficient, and profitable networkers in the world. While each and every one of them eats, breaths, speaks and truly believes in the power of networking, some of them were once doubters. Others did not know how to network effectively and were once a total mess, and are now a success. Some were the "victims" of what can only be called the "nightmares of networking."

Since I define networking as "the creation of new relationships and the enhancement of existing ones through engagement, for the purpose of mutual business and personal development," I believe that you will probably want to make a connection with some of the contributors. I would encourage you to first learn more about them in the *Contributors* section at the end of the book and also from their most up-to-date biographical information found on **www.worldsworstnetworker.com,** and reach out to them. Like the true master networkers they are, they will be more than happy to connect with you and to help you.

While every single one of these stories is true, behind every account are valuable lessons that were learned (in some cases, the hard way) by each of us. We are sharing these lessons with you so that you will know how to handle people, as well as similar situations you may find yourself in while networking. If you already think you are *The World's Worst Networker,* or if you can identify with any of the accounts, attitudes or behaviors that are profiled you will have the tools necessary to stop and correct your course before finding yourself and your business the subject of negative word-of-mouth.

-- Tim Houston

Contents

Section 4: From A Mess to A Success:
Strategies and Stories To Make You a Better Networker

Section 1:
The Most Unwanted List

"Networking is simple, but it's not easy. If it were easy, everyone would do it, and do it well. But not everyone does."

Ivan Misner, Ph.D., David Alexander &

Brian Hilliard.

Networking Like a Pro:

Turning Contacts into Connections

While *The World's Worst Networker* can come in many forms, the characters, charmers and clowns that are chronicled here are typically found in most situations and are indeed the worst of the worst. **Beware and be aware of them!**

Chapter 1

The Trader

Bob Burg

I believe that before we can discuss what people might do wrong when Networking, we first need to be on the same page regarding what Networking is and what it isn't.

While I define Networking as "The cultivating of mutually beneficial, *give* and take, win/win relationships" (the emphasis on the give part), you'll find that most other known authorities in this genre and in this book, including Tim Houston, Dr. Ivan Misner, Susan RoAne, Robyn Henderson, etc. all see it similarly, even if they define it with different words.

What Networking isn't…is the very thing many people who have not studied this concept think it is; a way to "connect" with as many people as possible in such a way that you can get as much as you can from them. And – as the thought goes – if I must do something for them first, so be it; at least they will then owe me.

Of course, that's not Networking; that's trading. That's keeping score; tit for tat, this for that, and if I scratch your back, you'd better be ready to scratch mine, or you'll never get your back scratched in this town again!

I was reminded of this, when years ago when I was in a local direct selling business, I was looking for a product for a client that was turning out to be rather difficult to find. Suddenly, a person I indirectly knew and who was aware of the situation offered me a suggestion; an excellent suggestion.

I thanked him profusely. He then responded by letting me know that should his suggestion result in a sale he would appreciate a referral fee.

After agreeing with him, a mental note was then made in my mind that this was not a person I wanted to do business with if at all possible. Not because I minded paying him a referral fee, but because of the very fact he asked for one showed me that he did not have my best interests, nor the best interests of my client in mind; he was thinking of himself and only himself.

Now, one might ask, "but, isn't that natural?" Sure it is. As human beings we certainly are – and should be – interested in ourselves. However, it just so happens that the best Networkers are willing to, as British author Thomas Power puts it, "temporarily suspend their self-interest."

Not forgo it, mind you. Just suspend it. Suspend it long enough that you can genuinely and authentically put the other person's interests first – yes, the other person's interests first! Do this, and you'll find yourself attracting other successful Networkers into your life and into your business. Successful people operate this way. They understand that when you genuinely care about the other person; *their* wants, *their* needs, *their* desires, you plant seeds of goodwill – of *great* will – that continually take root and sprout.

The gentleman helped me . . . for a price. Had he not made

that demand, not only would I have respected him a lot more. I'd have gone out of my way to provide value for him – much more than he provided for me. Had he been taught to network effectively, he would have desired to continue doing that for me and for others in his world.

Networking the correct way causes a rising tide that lifts all ships. Everyone's! Trading, on the other hand, at best keeps things as they are; at worst creates a tide of suspicion and distrust.

Give because you love to give. Provide value to people's lives because that's just what you do. And, as you do this, you'll see your own tide of abundance rise significantly.

Chapter 2

The Schnorrer

Tim Houston

At various points in our lives, we have all met someone who wanted something for nothing. Whether it was the person who wanted the "free gift" for just stopping in your store, or the person who asked to "borrow" a pen, a book or a few dollars, without any intention of ever giving it back to you.

We commonly refer to these people as "freeloaders" or moochers". When it comes to networking, the Yiddish word, "Schnorrer" (pronounced SHNOR-ur) is more fitting as it is one of Yiddish's worst epithets.

According to The Random House Dictionary, a Schnorrer, is defined as "a person who habitually borrows or lives at the expense of others with no intention of repaying; sponger; moocher; beggar."

One of the most popular Schnorrers is the character of Wimpy in the classic cartoon and comic strip series *Popeye*. Wimpy is very intelligent and well educated, but also very lazy, overly parsimonious and utterly gluttonous. He is also something of a scam artist and, especially in the newspaper strip, can be notoriously underhanded at times[1]. His most famous line is that

---

[1] See "J. Wellington Wimpy." *Wikipedia, the Free Encyclopedia*. 13 Oct. 2010. Web. 8 Dec. 2010.

he will "gladly pay you Tuesday for a hamburger today."

As it relates to networking, JewishDictionary.com gives a more accurate example of this type of the World's Worst Networker:

> "In contrast to the ordinary house-to-house beggar, whose business is known and easily recognized, The Schnorrer assumes a gentlemanly appearance, disguises his purpose, gives evasive reasons for asking assistance, and is not satisfied with small favors, being indeed quite indignant when such are offered[2]."

Over the years and at almost every event, I have encountered many a Schnorrer but one whom I'll call "Dr. Max" fits this definition almost too perfectly.

My Encounter with The Schnorrer

It was one of the hottest days of the year. I was exhibiting at one of the largest business expos in New York City which was held at CitiField, home of the New York Mets. Thankfully, it was indoors!

By 3:00 pm, most of the attendees had left and the majority of the exhibitors were starting to take down their

---

<http://en.wikipedia.org/wiki/J._Wellington_Wimpy>.
[2] Jacobs, Joseph, and Judah David Einstein. "- SCHNORRER." *JewishEncyclopedia.com*. Web. 13 Oct. 2010 <http://www.jewishencyclopedia.com/view.jsp?artid=344&letter=S>.

displays. I still had six people at my booth, talking to me about the various training programs, books and CDs I offer to my clients. I also had a few promotional pens that were left on my table for attendees to take.

As I was finishing my conversation, I noticed this scholarly looking gentleman in a tweed jacket on the other side of the room looking in my direction. Around his neck was strapped a press-credentials badge along with a camera. He was milling about, taking pictures of the venue and whatever few exhibitors were left. I thought I had seen him earlier in the day but I couldn't exactly recall.

After the last person left my booth, my assistants and I began packing up our stuff to leave. My two assistants said that they would be taking some of our stuff downstairs to load the car as the elevators were filled to capacity. We had a very long day and an even longer drive back home.

As my assistants left, the gentleman with the press badge came over to my table. With camera in hand, he shouted "SMILE!" as he took my picture.

"Hi, I'm Dr. Maximilian Spaulding, but call me Dr. Max. I am a writer and a talk show host. Who are you?"

I introduced myself, and briefly told him about how I helped business people to become more productive, profitable and prosperous through business networking. I asked him what he was he a doctor of, and which publications he wrote for.

Dr. Max said he was a "doctor of philosophy in

communications" and he began to name several out-of-town, publications and radio stations I had never heard of. He said they were small, but well-listened and well-read. This struck me as odd, so I asked him why he was covering a local event many miles away from the base of his readership.

"Well, I cover stories of interest for our readers. Going to expos like this, I find people that they would be interested in learning about and I write about them in my columns or interview them on my radio show." He said this as he took a few of the remaining promotional pens from my table.

"Mr. Houston, being a very successful, educated businessman, you probably know that it takes money to put on a show. Perhaps you or some of the many people you know could be sponsors for my radio show. Can you give me the names of some people I could contact?" He said this as he clicked one of the pens he had previously taken from my table and pulled out a pad, (a promotional item that was given away by another exhibitor at the expo).

Although he was ready to take down names and phone numbers of my contacts, I politely explained to Dr. Max that since we just met, I couldn't introduce him to my contacts. I thought to myself, "I never heard of his show or read any of his works. He's crazy to think I'm going to introduce him to the people I know." I asked if he could provide me with a website or some information so I could review his work.

Apparently annoyed, he reached inside his pocket and

produced a bent and wrinkled card saying "After your done checking me out, maybe you will want to give me a call with those names," as he thrust his card into my hand. He quickly walked away and disappeared down the hall in the direction of the elevators just as my assistants were returning.

Getting Something for Nothing

We finished packing up what was left of our belongings and were exhausted. We were among the last to leave the exhibit hall; walking into the parking lot and into what felt like a wall of heat. In my hand I had the last copy of my CD, *10 Techniques to Master Networking.*

As we were approaching my car, there was Dr. Max about to get into his car which was coincidentally parked in the same row a few spots from mine. He saw us as we began to load the car and made his way over. Seeing the mentally and physically exhausted state I was in, he made his move.

"Mr. Houston, can I ask you a question about the CD that you are holding? Was that the same one you had on your table before?"

"Yes it was for sale earlier today," I replied.

"Can you tell me what is it about?"

I told him it was a program that I recorded called the *10 Techniques to Master Networking* that serves as a guide to help people in various networking situations.

"Do you think it would be a good resource for me to learn

more about you if I wanted to interview you for a story or a radio interview?"

"It could," I said, "but I think to get to know me better, it would be best for us to talk or to meet. Of course you can visit my website, **www.tmhouston.com** to learn more about me as well."

"You know, if I had the CD, it would be so much easier for me to come up with questions for our interview..."

Interrupting him, I said, "If you wanted a copy of the CD, all you had to do was ask."

Unmasked!

In a somewhat apologetic rage, he said, "No! No! No! It's not that I *want* the CD *for myself.* Look, being a *Ph.D.,* a *radio show host, a columnist for several papers*, and with all the traveling I do, it's almost impossible for me to sit down and talk to you over coffee. But if I evaluated the CD and reviewed it positively on my show, then I could have you as my guest and in good-faith, endorse you."

Now I really recognized him for who he was and what he really wanted – and I wanted him gone. But because I was so hot and tired, I just went over and gave the CD to him.

"Dr. Max, here, take the CD, as my *gift* to you," I said.

"Mr. Houston, I wouldn't call it a gift as so much as a necessity for me to help boost your image. I will call you tomorrow after I listen to the CD to set up an interview and I will email the photo I took of you," he said as he walked back to his car, got in and drove away.

One of my assistants Ivan Radujko who is from Serbia looked at me and said, "Why did you give him a free CD?" I replied that I just wanted to get the guy away from me. I then briefly explained to Ivan what had happened inside the expo while he was away.

"You do know that guy was going around to everyone's tables today and was talking to them and took whatever samples he could get from them. He reminded me of the gypsies I've seen in Belgrade and throughout Europe, but without the begging." said Ivan.

"No Ivan, he's not a gypsy. He's what's known as a Schnorrer, one of the most annoying kind and one of the worst networkers in the world. They're all about themselves. They believe in getting but never giving. I'm not expecting anything to come out of this."

I was right. Dr. Max never called me the next day, nor the next week or month. For laughs, I emailed and called him a few times without any success. I wasn't going to ask for an interview I just wanted a copy of the photo he took of me. Needless to say, I never got a reply from him.

The Not Worker

A Schnorrer doesn't see the need or believe in the wealth of creating relationships. They know that relationships require people to be genuine – something that they are usually not. A Schnorrer appears more important than they are, often with an air of superiority to others. They brag about their degrees and how professional they are – and how they can be even more successful with access to your personal, financial and social resources.

They view networking as they view life: they are to come back with something – anything – at no expense to them. It usually starts off with obtaining something small, and then increases to much bigger things. Just like Wimpy, Dr. Max "won" that day by getting something from me. While it was just a CD, I can only imagine if he scored a bigger "win" from others, who were lured into his promises of an interview "tomorrow" which probably never came.

At networking events, The Schnorrer is more of a "not-worker." He or she will whine, guilt and cajole people into taking action to give them what they want. They will stay in your presence and spend a great deal of your time and energy in the hopes of getting something from you – a referral, a contact, perhaps even a something as a complimentary admission to an event – while spending very little, if any of their time and money in return.

Just Say No!

My approach to dealing with Schnorrers is simple: move away from them as far as you can. The goal is not to become their victim by "helping them out." The best advice I can give you is to just say no. While you do not have to be rude, when a Schnorrer becomes apparent and asks you for something, tell them that you're sorry but you cannot help them and that you are sure that they can figure it out or get it on their own.

The goal is not to show the slightest interest in helping them; otherwise it will just feed into their Academy Award winning performance. You cannot let these parasites leach onto you or to find a way to make you feel sympathetic or "sorry" for them. They don't care and won't care about you now or ever. If you have any Schnorrers in your life, do what you can to purge them because no matter what you do for them it will never be enough.

Remember, good networking is a two-way street where both parties give and take (in a good way), and that helps to move the relationship along. With The Schnorrer, it's just a one-way street where they always take and take and take, often ending in a dead-end for their victim.

Chapter 3

Distributors And Collectors
Of Business Cards

Tony Wolfe

There are two huge, often made mistakes that people will make while networking. This error automatically puts them in the category of *The World's Worst Networker;* they are distributors and collectors of business cards. Some even treat it like a contest to see how many of their cards they can hand out and how many cards they can collect from others.

What is the purpose behind this activity? How productive is it? What else could you have been doing with your time that would have provided you with much greater results?

Before you give out your next business card, consider someone having your card as a privilege – *for them.* Your card is something that *you* decide to give out based on your relationship with them. Don't just deal them out as if you were playing a game of poker. You need to consider things such as how well do you know them? How much you trust them? What can you provide for them and what can they provide for you? Much of this can be established in the initial conversation – assuming you actually have one, because most distributors and collectors don't!

As we examine the behavior of these two types of

networkers through some examples, think about your own activity at networking events and how you can improve your networking skills.

The Distributor

Picture this: you are at a networking event and you've spotted Card Guy. He's named "Card Guy" not because he sells cards, but because his idea of networking is shoving his business card into the hands and faces of as many people as he can manage at almost every networking event in town.

The conversations he has with those who are victimized by him very seldom last more than a minute. He walks away thinking, "Wow! I just made a great contact!" The victim gladly watches him walk away and thinks, "Wow! What a goof ball."

We've probably all seen that type of "networking". How well does that work? For most, it does not work very well at all.

The business card is perhaps one of the most misused tools in the business world. For many people it creates an assumption that just because the card has been passed it means that business will actually take place. That is simply not true.

Card Guy lacks some skills and knowledge about how to effectively network. When it comes to passing along the contact information (your business card), be very selective. This is counter intuitive as most people believe that the more people who have your card the more exposure you and your company get. While this is true to a degree, however, when you are meeting someone for the first time and you shove your card at them before you take the time to learn something about them, it makes you appear desperate for business. This is probably not the image you wanted to create as your first impression.

Remember, there is positive exposure and negative exposure. What are you striving to achieve?

The passing of the card should be done at the end of the conversation as part of your wrap up. This is after you have learned enough about them to decide that you want to stay in contact with them and learn more about them. Hopefully, they will feel the same way about you. Remember to always ask permission to offer your card. Don't just assume they want it.

To an extent, whenever you pass along your card, you are passing along some of your trust. You are making a statement to the person to whom you have given the card. You are saying to them, "Our initial interaction was positive and I would like to communicate more. Here is my contact information and I look forward to our next conversation."

As you walk away smiling and they are also smiling, you have accomplished something that Card Guy only wishes he had the ability to accomplish. You don't just have a business card: you have the beginning of a relationship. You must now nurture it and give it the proper attention so as to allow it the time to mature into that mutually beneficial relationship that you were shooting for from the start.

The Collector

Card Guy is back! He is handing out his cards like a madman (as always). He is also collecting as many as he can. He takes his catch for the day back to his office and neatly inserts the cards into a card file. He leans back in his chair and takes pride in his new additions to his collection of cards. (He is, after all, Card Guy!)

Wonderful! Now what? They sit there...and they sit there...and do a little more sitting there. (Isn't this exciting?!) As he looks at the literally hundreds and hundreds of business cards in those files, he foolishly thinks to himself, "I am probably the best connected businessman in this city!" It would be painful for him to know that, in fact, he is not.

If you gathered up all of the business cards that you have in your office, car, briefcase, etc. and took an inventory of them, how many of those people would you actually know? Not just know who they are, but *really know* them. How many of those business professionals would you call upon if you needed their product or service or better yet, knew someone who did? Would you remember that you have the card?

If you began to throw out all of the cards of the people who you could not identify in a lineup, you would probably throw away a vast majority of your collection. But what are you really losing? You don't know them, which probably means they don't know you either. Start tossing!

Having someone's card does not establish or define a

relationship. Them having your card doesn't establish anything either. The exchange of this powerful business tool should be done with care and respect.

Content of a Business Card

What does your card have on it? Hopefully it contains your business name, perhaps a logo, an address, phone number, a fax number, an email address and a website. It's your calling card so people can contact you. Make it easy for that to happen when *they* want to make it happen.

Why would you hand out a business card (used to allow people to contact you) and not provide them with the information so that they can do that? How much energy and time do you want them to spend trying to track you down? They will more than likely go elsewhere if they have to spend time hunting for your information. When trying to attract clients or referral sources, the ability to contact you is a key component in the process. Make it clear and easy for them.

Your success in business will be a direct result of your relationships with others. If you take the time to build carefully from the very start, you will have surrounded yourself with great contacts and sources.

Remember, it can start with just a conversation and your business card.

Chapter 4

The Wanderer

Tim Houston

It was in 2001while I was attending a networking meeting that I was introduced to Carl. Carl was a salesperson with a national communications company that was rapidly expanding its wireless communications products and plans, with a focus on business customers. Because Carl's niche market was small business owners and outside sales people who relied upon cell phones, he told me that networking events and organizations would be a great place for him to get qualified referrals for his business. At the event, Carl was the only wireless salesperson in attendance, so people naturally drifted in his direction to hear about what his company had to offer.

Two weeks later, I found myself at another networking event, across town. To my surprise, there was Carl. Carl had an opportunity to speak for about a minute to the attendees about his company's products and services. By the end of the event, Carl was standing with an audience surrounding him, listening to his every word and wanting to know more as he was being showered with business cards from everyone in sight.

After the throng of people left, I walked over to Carl and reintroduced myself, reminding him that we met a few weeks before. I asked him if he had any intention of becoming a part of the organization which sponsored the event where we met. Carl said he had to think about it to ensure he would get a good return on his investment. When I told him that he could probably get more referrals if he participated as a member instead of a guest, he replied that he believed it would be better for him not to stay in one place. He felt that his product was the best and the group we were talking about only represented a tiny percentage of the business people in the county who "needed" his phones.

A month after that event, I was speaking to a friend named Liz who ran a referral group in another county. Her group had about 35 members, and we were talking about the people who recently visited over the past month. Lo and behold, Carl's name was on the list. Liz said that her group was looking to refer business to a wireless sales rep and she thought Carl would be an ideal candidate and asked if I knew him.

"Do you remember the song 'The Wanderer' by Dion and the Belmonts?" I asked.

"Yes but what do you mean?" my friend said.

"Well Carl is a Wanderer. Like the song says '[He's] the type of guy that likes to roam around, he's never in one place, he roams from town to town...'."

"Tim, I think he's going to settle down now. Besides he applied to be a part of our group."

"I'll bet you lunch that he won't last more than 2 months with you, let alone refer anyone business. Guys like him go to groups and networking events and try to sell people instantly. Some will buy, others won't. I'm telling you that guys like him don't plant their roots let alone care about building relationships."

"We'll see. He's good at what he does and I think maybe he's had a change of heart since he is applying for membership," Liz retorted, as she accepted my bet.

In the end, I lost the bet. **Carl lasted 2 months and 2 weeks and then moved on.** After Carl sold his phones to as many people in the group as he could, he quit.

I called Carl to find out why he left the group. He told me that he believed that he would still get referrals from those he sold the phones to. Besides, the phones were so hot, *they sold themselves*. I asked Carl if he honestly believed that and he said he did. I asked Carl if he had a chance to get to know anyone in the group to which he replied that he didn't have time to really spend with anyone, let alone attending the weekly meetings. Besides, he boasted that he **made over $5,000 in commissions** just by going to these networking meetings for a few months.

Carl's story doesn't end there. Before we continue, you need to know exactly the group of networkers that Carl belonged to: Carl was a bona fide Wanderer.

The Wanderer is one of *The World's Worst Networkers* in many respects because they are not focused on networking at all. Instead, they are focused on one thing: just making the sale and making it fast. Wanderers have been around for ages in many societies. Some take the form of nomads, traveling across desserts, following their herds and never settling down. Others go about from town to town, peddling their wares, like the popular traveling salesman of the early 20th Century, or like the dubious "snake oil peddlers" who hawked their "cures" at popular traveling medicine shows during the late half of the 19th Century in America.

The Signs:

As can be seen by Carl's action and words, Wanderers tend to come to events – sometimes out of desperation and other times out of motivation – rarely with the intent of staying for the long haul. Carl joined one networking group and was gone within a short period of time after he believed that all of his prospects were exhausted. Little did Carl know that he would have made a lot more money and could have received more referrals had he the knowledge, patience and true sincerity of wanting to help others instead of helping himself.

So how do you know if someone is a Wanderer? Besides seeing them in many places, they approach their victim with a very strong sense of urgency to the point where the victim feels pressured. Sometimes they will say that their products won't be available very long; other times they will outright tell you that they are just "passing through" and this is a "once in a lifetime opportunity."

If you are in a networking group, when a Wanderer meanders in and tries to sell to the group or solicit referrals, the best defense is for the group to say:

"We will be happy to consider referring business to you

and possibly doing business with you, but you need to show a long-term commitment to our group by applying for membership."

The Wanderer will hopefully get the message and either leave or apply for membership. If they do apply, extra care and caution during the screening process must be taken to ensure that this Wanderer, is, indeed, going to settle down.

As the late Paul Harvey would say, *"And now the rest of the story...."*

Fast forward to 2005. I was hired to conduct a seminar on strategic networking for a group of sales people at a major life insurance company. In discussing the value of networking to form long-term relationships, I related the story about Carl the Wanderer to the audience, (without mentioning his name). As I am teaching this important lesson, I looked out into the audience and I could see that in the fourth row was Carl The Wanderer, playing with his Blackberry!

I didn't get a chance to speak to Carl that day as he was one of the first people to leave the room. About two years later, I was hired again by that same life insurance company to teach some of their new hires. Remembering Carl had worked there, I asked about him. Most people I met did not know who Carl was, but I found out that one person, a manager, did remember him. He told me that Carl left the company about a month after he attended my seminar, saying that he didn't "have the time" to network.

Lessons learned:

Carl The Wanderer taught me a valuable lesson. The best networkers are like giant redwood trees that plant their roots very deep in order to grow tall, while providing protection and an environment for other species to thrive. On the other hand, Wanderers are like lonely tumbleweeds in the desert, rolling along consuming the moisture and nutrients of the soil (i.e. the people and groups they come into contact with) and creating significant damage to the soil, (in this case, they burn bridges and lose credibility which destroys their reputation).

I don't know whatever became of Carl, but I do know that Carl was no longer a regular at the various networking events that people used to see him attend. Perhaps Carl wandered on to "the next big thing." Maybe he gave up sales altogether or wandered on to another town, looking for yet another opportunity to perform a "hit and run" sale. In the end, I don't think Carl ever got the message or ever will.

Chapter 5

Nasty, Up-Close-And-Personal, Pushy Good 'Ole Boy

Weston Lyon

Without question, the absolute worst networker I've ever witnessed was a nasty, up-close-and-personal, good 'ole boy insurance agent named Jerry. In a moment, I'll explain why I believe Jerry is *The World's Worst Networker*; but first I'd like to give you a little background info on how I know Jerry and about the interactions I've had with him.

I met Jerry about 7 years ago at a networking event, which we both later joined. Inside the group he represented his insurance company. I had the "privilege" of spending 3 years witnessing Jerry's unusual network skills before parting ways.

In that time together, here are some peccadilloes I personally observed. [**WARNING**: some may not be for the faint of heart]:

1. **Nasty Displays of Affection** – On more than a dozen occasions Jerry felt it necessary to 'pass gas' while networking with others. The majority of those pleasurable experiences were when the members of the group (myself included) sat down next to Jerry for part of the meeting. No "excuse me" or "pardon me" talk. Just a nod and a smile…like we enjoyed him doing it!?!

Needless to say, after an episode of flatulence, I never sat directly next to Jerry again. I made sure to always be at a distance from smelling him but unfortunately, never far enough away from hearing him.

2. **Personal Space Takeover** -- Yes, Jerry was the type of person who would stand 3 inches away from your face while speaking to you.

He had no regard for his morning coffee breath or your personal space. His conversations with you were always up close and personal. Too close. And if that weren't enough, Jerry had a bit of a problem when it came to controlling his saliva attack. You got it: an onslaught of spittle. And there was nothing you could do about it once he had you "in range."

3. **Push, Push, Push**- Jerry was also of the mindset of the 'Good Ole Boys.' You know. The kind of people who try to buy your business with a few drinks.

He engaged in the kind of sales tactics that pushed people away instead of attracting them. He had the kind of attitude that's all-take-no-give. Always selfish and never generous.

His approach was to be upfront, in-your-face; the one that says "Buy from me, only from me and buy from me **now**! If not now – WHEN!?!"

You see, I told you Jerry was *The* World's *Worst Networker*. Of course, this is just my opinion. Instead of just calling Jerry out, let's take a look at what we can learn from Jerry's nasty, up-close-and-personal, good 'ole boy behaviors and how we can make adjustments to become better networkers ourselves.

1. **Be Courteous** – You would think this one doesn't need to be explained; but let's face it, some people are just nasty. Be courteous. Don't do anything at a networking event you wouldn't do at home while entertaining guests you've never had at your home. Your friends may put up with you and your 'nasty behaviors', but strangers shouldn't have to.

2. **Become Aware** – Notice the reaction of the person you're talking to as you get closer to their own personal space. Everyone's different. Some will let you get as close as 6 inches before acting differently; while others get nervous when you get within 2 feet. Respect their distance. Become aware of where they get uncomfortable. (Trust me…you'll know when. They'll go from a relaxed state to looking like they're constipated. It's not hard to notice when you're paying attention).

3. **Wake Up** – If you haven't noticed, everything looks different today compared to 20 years ago. Same is true for networking. Wake up! Networking today isn't about making the sale! It's about building relationships and developing trust. It's about getting to know one another and giving without expecting in return.

Networking has changed. Change with it. Understand what it is and where it's going and, how you can embody its nature and philosophy.

So, is Jerry *The World's Worst Networker*? I think so...but get beyond my opinion. The real benefit is in looking and observing what others, like Jerry, do...and do the opposite!

Learn from the world's worst...and become your personal best!

Chapter 6

The Slick Hunter

LuAnn Buechler, CMP

As a meeting and event planner, a co-organizer of an annual networking event in the United States called *Get Connected* and as a director for the world's largest business networking organization, BNI, I meet hundreds – if not thousands – of people each year. Most people are extremely nice and professional, but there are always some who make me shake my head in amazement, wondering to myself, "How do they survive in business?"

One such person was a salesman that sold oil to individuals or mechanics for use in cars and other machinery. Since he proved himself to be such an awful networker, I'll refer to him as Slick Willie.

Slick Willie appeared at a special Visitors Day event held by a BNI chapter in Minnesota. I had a chance to have a brief conversation with Willie, during which he told me that he would never join just one network. His master plan was to visit all the chapters and networking organizations he could to find business. When he was done, he would move on to the next city. As a director for BNI, I was supporting 4 chapters in our city at the time; so I saw Willie on several occasions and Willie definitely saw me.

Months later, at the end of one particular meeting, Willie came over to me and said "I was told you are the person who can help me to network."

"I am," I replied.

"You seem to know everyone, so if you will do business with me, you can spread the message about how great my product is," he said. I inquired again if he planned to join a chapter and got the same response. "No, why would I do that. I am going to visit them all to get business, and then move on to the next city."

Willie proceeded to tell me all about his oil: how he could come to my home to put it in my car and also teach me how to do it, etc. I told Willie, I only business with people I know, like and trust. "If you plan to join BNI, we can build that relationship and talk more about your products and services." Willie again expressed his views on networking, and how he did not have time to build those relationships. "Trust me; it's a great product, just try it and you'll see. You have my word." Willie said.

I explained to Willie, "…part of the value of BNI to me is doing business with people I know that I can trust. I know nothing about cars and honestly have no desire to learn. I work with a mechanic who I have built a relationship with to the point that I trust him implicitly with my cars. I would never do anything to my car without Jerry's input." I told him, if he wanted to speak to Jerry about his oil products I would connect him. I made the mistake of mentioning the name of Jerry's business – a slip that would later come back to haunt me.

He assured me that was unnecessary. "Well, I only do business with Jerry and unless Jerry tells me this is the oil I need and encourages me to put it in my car, I will not be buying oil from you directly." Slick Willie was quite persistent; he wanted to go in the parking lot to put oil in my car. To end the conversation, I had to tell Willie I had another meeting with several people who were waiting patiently for me, and needed to go.

Hours later, I felt the need to call Jerry to warn him about my conversation earlier that morning. Jerry was pleased to hear from me. I started the conversation by saying "Jerry, I called to warn you about a guy I spoke to this morning..."

Jerry interrupted: "LuAnn, he's already been here."

I was speechless for a moment. Jerry then informed me that Willie had gone to his shop and told him that *I* sent him there; that *I* wanted the oil in my car and that Jerry needed to buy his oil in order to take care of his customers, especially *me*. I felt so used, betrayed, humiliated and ashamed that Slick Willie had entered my network and started to tell outright lies! I began to apologize profusely to Jerry for ever having mentioned his name to Slick Willie.

Fortunately, Jerry and I have a very strong business relationship which we developed through our BNI chapter. Jerry knew better than to listen to Slick Willie. When Willie insisted, Jerry kept his cool and said "Let me speak to LuAnn. If she wants your oil I will get it for her. However, what I have been using in her vehicles is what I would still recommend to her."

Willie continued by trying to sell Jerry some oil, assuring him I would want it. Jerry knew better and sent Willie on his way.

I felt so badly that Jerry had to deal with Slick Willie because of my slip of the tongue. Jerry reassured me that it was because of our relationship and how well he knew me, that this incident was no reflection on me. He was confident that Willie was lying to him and that I had never really sent Willie there to sell Jerry oil to put in my car. Jerry continued to reassure me that by word-of-mouth, he was familiar with Willie and his tactics so there was no need to worry.

The Lesson I Learned:

My experience with Slick Willie proved to me that networking is about cultivating relationships. It is about farming rather than hunting. What Slick Willie didn't want to understand was that building a relationship and trust takes time. Jerry has been working on my cars for nearly 5 years and has earned my trust over time.

Slick Willie expected me to trust him based on one conversation and "his word." A great networker knows that their word is only the beginning. It is like the seeds that are planted which will grow into an abundant harvest, if properly watered and cared for. Great networkers know that they must prove themselves to their networking partners in order to nurture those relationships. This can be done simply by taking the time to meet their partners in a one-to-one situation in order to get a better understanding of each other's' business.

It means taking the time to build the relationship to the point of trusting each other implicitly where they can continuously refer business to one another. When business is referred, the great networkers will treat the prospects (i.e. those people that are referred by a trusted partner) with the utmost respect and sincerity and deliver the products and services they have committed to in their "word", creating mutually beneficial results for all: the prospect, the source of the referral and the receiver of the referral.

> *"Be true to your work, your word and your friends."*
> **– Henry David Thoreau**

Because Jerry and I live by the relationship we have built and do business based on trust, Jerry truly "had my back" in that situation. Willie was a very slick hunter. He set his sights on a target and was coming in for the kill. Willie proved that he was unethical and a liar, and would do anything to "make the sale." Slick Willie, and other networking hunters like him will never come between, use or deceive the solid relationships that I have with my networking partners.

Chapter 7

The Instant Winner

Mike Morrison

Networking is becoming a massive part of people's marketing strategies. With the change in the economy and the change in attitudes, it has brought forth a change in the way we do business. More and more people are realizing we are living in a world of engagement, rather than in interruption. Engaging with potential customers is much more effective than interrupting them with sales pitches and advertising.

Because this shift has occurred more recently, you still have many people who have an "old school" mentality with outdated views when it comes to networking. These types of bad networkers are the people who turn up to networking events, chat with a few people in the room and then declare that they need to be around people who are from "bigger businesses." They believe that the smaller business represented in the room are not valuable to them – a very deadly mistake.

In addition, you also see the people who are in the room that go to two or three networking events a week or month. At the end of each month, they sit down with a spreadsheet to see how much they have spent and how much they have earned, and try to figure out their "return of investment" on their networking efforts.

Networking doesn't work like that. It is not about "instant wins." Networking is about cultivating relationships and keeping a steady stream of awareness about you, your business and what you offer. It makes it easier for people to approach you when they need your services, but even more importantly (and better) when they pass along your details to someone that they know who wants the very product or service that you offer.

If you're after "instant wins" you are better off buying a scratch-off lottery ticket. You may as well stand all day at the cash-register at a supermarket or a lottery agent buying one scratch-off after another. Sure, you may get lucky and win some "big money" but you may also spend $2 and only win $1. Given the odds, the chances are you will be worse off than you started.

Networking, marketing and business in general is not about "instant wins." The problem is that people expect networking to be instantly profitable because every once in a while, someone goes into a networking event or they apply a marketing tactic and that generates an instant result. They may have met someone, given them a sales pitch, and *voilà*, that person becomes a client.

Then, the next time they go to a networking event and try the same thing, nothing happens. They then conclude (wrongfully) that "networking doesn't work." What they do not realize is on that one occasion they got lucky. Just as purchasing dozens of scratch-off, instant-win lottery tickets, every day, would not be a sound financial strategy, going to a few networking events and expecting "instant results" is a foolish business strategy.

We live in an era of engagement marketing, where banging out sales pitches and looking for immediate returns simply no longer works. Today, the onus is on connecting and engaging with those around you in order to develop fruitful business relationships. Engagement needs to happen in your online and offline networking efforts. It requires you to have patience, to listen, respect, and respond to others, instead of dictating what you want them to do. You cannot expect, like the "instant winners" do, that people will automatically become your client or refer you some business just but for the sake of giving a referral – or even worse, just because you showed up to the event.

So, whether you are new to the world of networking or have been in it for a while and may be wondering why you're not getting more positive results, take notice of your mindset, your expectations, and how you approach your networking. At the next networking event you go to or the next time you log into a social media site, keep an eye out for those people who are simply chasing instant wins. If you find yourself doing the same thing, put on the breaks and **STOP!** Then restart with a new approach and attitude that networking is a slow-race which is to be won when the relationships are first built, blossom, become strengthened and then thrive, resulting in more business for everyone.

Chapter 8

The Self-Absorbed, "Expert Networker"

Susan RoAne

Most of us are not natural networkers. Some who think they are, even so-called experts, often prove themselves to be just the opposite. Case in point: "Renee" was approached by a literary agent to write a book on networking, a topic for which she was well-known. Due to contract restrictions with a current publisher, Renee couldn't accept the offer but, as a natural networker, she recommended "Debbie," a colleague, who also spoke and wrote on the topic. The agent didn't know Debbie so Renee provided Debbie's contact information as well as an enthusiastic recommendation. She called Debbie to give her the "heads-up." The deal was sealed. But Debbie never called or wrote Renee to say thank you.

This lack of networking savvy and manners was a tip off to Renee that something was missing in this expert's skill set. So when she saw Debbie at a conference, Renee mentioned the book and asked that she be quoted as the "thank you." If you don't ask, the clueless (or thoughtless) can't say yes. Debbie sweetly agreed.

Eight months later Renee realized Debbie hadn't been in touch to solicit/confirm a quote, so she called her. Debbie became flustered and said the manuscript was already finished. Renee was stunned. Debbie started to backpedal and told Renee that she had known the agent before, implying that Renee's

36

matchmaking was irrelevant. Renee asked Debbie, if that were true, why did she have to tell the agent who Debbie was and give her Debbie's contact information?

The very savvy networker in this situation was Renee. She couldn't do the project, so she (1) tried to help the agent find a substitute; (2) made the referral, provided the recommendation and shared Debbie's contact information. Here is what sets apart the savvy from the self-absorbed, (3) Renee called Debbie to give her the heads-up about the agent so she would be prepared when she received the agent's call. Debbie, someone who was known for her networking presentations, either didn't practice what she preached or wasn't well-versed in all levels of the process that, to me, are common sense and common courtesy. There was no "thank you" for the lead, nor did she follow through on her own promise to quote Renee as the "payback" acknowledgment until Renee reminded her of their conversation.

It's not enough to say you're a networking expert. One must be savvy and have great command of the nuances of networking. Behavior, deeds and actions, as always, speak louder than words.

Chapter 9

The Outsourced Networker

Tim Houston

Outsourcing. The mere mention of the word will cause different reactions from different people. What was once seen as a cost-saving measure used by big companies – especially IT firms – the practice of outsourcing has truly changed the way business is conducted in a variety industries. While this practice remains extremely controversial and creates a firestorm of political debate as well as sharp differences in the public's opinion, the outsourcing of specific job functions – and even more so increasingly popular, daily-life functions such as doing daily errands – continues to grow. So it should come as no surprise that there are some people and businesses that have tried to "outsource" their networking efforts as well. Unfortunately, these attempts have always ended up with disastrous results.

The Revolving Door Approach to Networking:

I frequently speak before sales teams at conventions and conduct workshops for a variety of businesses. In 2001, I was asked to conduct a seminar for over 200 agents and sales managers at the New York City headquarters of one of the largest life insurance companies in the United States. While the company provided a top-notch sales training program which was the envy of the industry, the Vice President of the New York office wanted to help his agents and sales managers realize that they had to do more than just cold-call. He understood that even though billions of dollars were spent each year by his company on advertising, to stay competitive and to keep their clients, building relationships with members of the business community and developing new sources for qualified referrals were vital. I was asked to teach these agents how to network more productively beyond the "usual" business and social mixers. One of the central themes of the workshop was to encourage the agents to participate and engage in networking groups such as BNI in addition to their local Chambers of Commerce and service clubs like Rotary International or Kiwanis.

One young recently-promoted sales manager stood up during the question and answer portion of my presentation and boldly exclaimed that networking never produced any "real" results for her and it wasn't producing results for her team. She believed networking was a waste of time, proudly proclaiming that her agents should, like her, just "dial for dollars[3]" and solicit referrals from their "warm markets": their family members, friends and current clients. I decided to launch into a "failed networking autopsy" to see exactly what went wrong in her efforts.

What I discovered was that this sales manager ascribed to

---

[3] This was before the enactment of the "Do Not Call" law passed by Congress, when getting cold-calls was a common annoyance, especially at dinner and other inopportune moments.

the "revolving door" approach to networking. She would send one team member to represent her office at a Chamber's monthly business after hours event. The following month she would send a different one, never going herself. She joined a weekly networking group but the majority of the time, wouldn't attend and would just send another team member to substitute for her.

Like a revolving door, one person was coming in while another was going out. Should it be a big surprise that her networking efforts didn't work for her? After all, while some people knew about her and her sales office, no one could get to know *her* well enough to refer business to *her* with confidence. The mere fact that there was a different person representing her office at each event sent the wrong impression to the business community that her office had a high turn-over of personnel and thus it hurt the office's reputation.

> *"Appearances are often deceiving"*
> **– Aesop**

But it's not just the "big" companies who try to outsource their networking. Some small businesses have tried to do the same thing. In 2000, I was attending a networking event where I encountered no less than 20 financial advisors. I had a chance to talk to several of them but there was something about "Joe" that really stood out.

At first glance, he looked the part of a "typical" financial advisor: he was probably in his late 20s or early 30's, dressed conservatively in a suit and tie. When we met, he didn't have a business card. He explained that he just started with his company, a small local financial services firm, a week before. I asked Joe a question about the types of mutual funds his company offered for sale, expecting him to give me an answer containing the names of the funds from some of the bigger financial firms. Instead, his answer seemed like he was trying to dodge the question by telling me that he really didn't handle those and because he was relatively new, I would be better off speaking to someone else at his firm who would have more information. He then asked me a few questions about myself and my business, and then we parted.

A few months later, while I was at a local Chamber of Commerce business card exchange, I ran into Joe. Upon reintroducing myself, I jokingly reminded him that the first time we met, he didn't have a business card. This time he gave me a card which held the title "Client Relationship Manager". Bewildered, I said, "I thought you said you were a financial advisor" "Actually, I'm not. I don't have any of the licenses but I plan on getting them at some point in the future. The real financial advisor is my brother, and I'm working for his company in getting new clients. I go to these events to look for prospects or referral sources." When I asked why his brother didn't attend any events, Joe's reply was even more disturbing. "My brother is *too busy* and he *can't be bothered* going to weekly networking meetings or to Chamber events. He figured that he would send me instead."

> **"Meeting with people in person gives us an opportunity to truly connect with them."**
>
> **– Dr. Nano Pelusi, *Psychology Today***
> **November/December 2007**

One concept I teach to my seminar participants and to my clients is that people never do business with small businesses or giant companies; they do business with *other people*. In a survey of more than 2,200 Harvard Business Review subscribers, 95 percent said they believe that face-to-face meetings are key to success in building long-term relationships, and 87 percent agree face-to-face meetings are essential for "sealing the deal".[4]

The same is true with networking. In each of these cases what the sales manager and Joe didn't understand is that you cannot outsource your face-to-face networking activities the way a company would outsource their customer service center to a third party to manage and run. I also believe that the practice of "outsourcing" your social media networking is a bad idea – but that's a topic for another book.

People need to experience each other's personalities,

---

[4] *Managing Across Distance In Today's Economic Climate: The Value of Face-to-Face Communicatiions*. Working paper. Harvard Business Reveiw Analytic Services & British Airways. Web. 10 July 2009. <http://facetoface.ba.com/harvard-business-review.pdf>.

passions and knowledge. Just like romantic relationships cannot be built by proxy, one cannot effectively network by sending someone else to take their place, (but it doesn't stop them from trying).

Chapter 10

Cell Phone Commandos
Beth M. Anderson

The cell phone, the Blackberry™ the smart phone, instant messaging, text messaging, Skype™ and social networking. Never in the history of mankind has communication been easier, so fast and very efficient. But with progress and innovation comes responsibility: people need to remember their basic manners when using new technologies. Unfortunately, most people don't and that includes some business people who even use their cell phones to make calls, write emails and to send messages to friends while networking. I named this group of annoying networkers, the Cell Phone Commandos.

Ambushed!

Who amongst us has never experienced a cell phone ringing at an inappropriate time: be it at a movie, a family dinner, in church, or a museum. It's embarrassing when it turns out to be our phone, but when it comes to business or networking situations, it's even worse and extremely annoying when it is a person with whom we are giving our undivided attention to. Over the years, we have come to expect these things to happen but it still doesn't mean it's good manners and that people will not notice.

According to a study of done in the United States by research firm Synovate:

> "A surprising 70% of the population polled nationally observed people using technology in a manner that is disrespectful to others at least once a day.... [S]pecifically, 68% of the population sees the poorest etiquette with technology among cell phone users and 18% among email users." [5]

Cell Phone Commandos are among the World's Worst Networkers, because they believe that they must always be connected. If a call, email, text or instant message is missed, they believe that an opportunity may be passing them by. Depending on where they are situated, some Cell Phone Commandos will operate in a stealthy manner. If seated at a table or if in a meeting, they will make subtle glances downward, and will often fidget with their phone, in their lap or under the table as they checking email or replying to a message, every few minutes, hardly paying any attention to those around them. Other times, they will be more overt and reveal themselves within a manner of seconds of answering their phone and saying "hello," and completely forgetting the other people they are engaging with. In some cases, they will use their phones as a way or as an excuse to exit

---

[5] Synovate. "Snap out of It! You Likely Annoy Others Daily with Poor Manners with Technology." *Global Market Research | Synovate*. 26 July 2005. Web. 7 Sept. 2010. <http://www.synovate.com/news/article/2005/07/snap-out-of-it-you-likely-annoy-others-daily-with-poor-manners-with-technology.html>.

from a situation or conversation, thinking that the other people around them "will understand.".

Defensive Maneuvers

To prevent an ambush by a Cell Phone Commando, you do have a few defenses that are applicable in almost any situation. First, if you are in a group meeting, right at the outset, ask that everyone turn their phones off or set it to vibrate. You don't have to be authoritarian or rude in saying this. In fact, one particular networking group I know has an unofficial tradition in some of its chapters around the world: at the start of the meeting, the President asks everyone to turn off their phones, except all of those in the room who are celebrating a birthday, on that particular day. They warn, in a light-hearted, yet serious manner, that if a phone rings, they will stop everything they are doing and everyone in the room will sing "Happy Birthday" to the person whose phone rang.

Not only does this ensure that the meeting stays focused and on schedule, it neutralizes the Cell Phone Commando's ability to check their messages or take a call. In rare cases when a phone does ring, the Cell Phone Commando is a bit embarrassed because the person on the other end hears 20 to 50+ people singing "Happy Birthday". The other person will usually say they will call back later. Not only does a strong message get delivered, the message is understood and the Cell Phone Commando will think twice about not turning off their phone while in a meeting.

Another technique is to be very upfront and let everyone

you know that has a meeting scheduled with you that are you blocking out the time to dedicate your attention solely to them. Tell them that since their time and your time is valuable, you want the conversation to be productive, and ask them to shut off the cell phone. If you are having this meeting in your office, you should lead by example and turn off the ringer of your office phones or ask your receptionist to hold all of your calls. You can shut down your email as well; after all, who wants to hear dings or the computer telling you that you have new mail every thirty seconds? Do this in front of the Cell Phone Commando as it sets the stone for the rest of the meeting.

"Just Because You Can, Doesn't Mean You Should!"

Picture a meeting of 57 people, 53 of whom meet weekly to exchange business in a private room at a restaurant, seated around a very long U-shaped table arrangement, with white linen tablecloths. On this particular day, four other people from the business community were attending this meeting as invited guests to see this group and to decide if they wanted to apply for membership.

The meeting got underway, with the President standing and talking at one end of the room, welcoming everyone to the meeting. A few minutes into the meeting, a cell phone rings breaking his momentum and startling several people in the group. As people looked around to locate the culprit, one of the invited guests, a woman sitting within 6 feet of the President, bent over and started digging through her purse while the President raised his voice to talk above the ringing.

All of a sudden, she disappeared in plain sight of 56 people. She did not leave the room; instead, as if she was sneaking behind enemy lines, the Commando purposely *crawled under the table and answered her phone.* As if that wasn't bad enough, everyone heard her say, in a very chatty voice, *"Hi! How are you? It's been such a long time since we talked!"*

Bewildered, the President stopped for a moment, and looked at the empty chair. Was it an emergency? Probably not, since she continued to carry on speaking for another 30 seconds or so, chatting with what was obviously an acquaintance.

Eventually, the President got the meeting back on track, and kept speaking louder and louder until the Commando finally stopped talking and crawled back into her chair. As 112 eyes in the room just stared at her, she acted as if absolutely nothing had happened and continued on with the rest of the meeting, creating a very weird, uncomfortable feeling among the other 56 people in the room.

Credibility & Referability Killed in Action

Let's face it: we all have had times in our lives when we have felt like crawling under the table to hide. But when this particular Cell Phone Commando **actually did it, and more,** in front of a room of 56 other people, there was nothing she could have done to justify her actions. In no uncertain terms, she may have thought she was sending a message to everyone else that her call "was important" when in reality, the message she sent to everyone in the room was loud and clear: she did not think that they were as important as whoever it was on the other end of the phone. Her credibility diminished, her referability was reduced to almost zero and she embarrassed herself as well as the person who invited her to attend. I don't know if she applied for membership, but I do know that I never saw her again at any other networking meetings in the community.

Chapter 11

The 9 To 5 Networker

Tim Houston

Too often, business networking is thought of as something that people do when they are engaged in work-related activities. Many people think they can only network when attending cocktail parties, conferences, trade shows or within business organizations and only with other business people. After work ends, they believe that their networking has stopped until they go back to work the next day.   These "9 to 5" Networkers overlook one of their best resources for new contacts as well as potential referrals: their family and friends.

Many people believe the old saying "never do business with family or friends;" in fact, the 9 to 5 Networker wears this saying on their sleeve. However, because of my own personal experiences and observations, I have found that most people cannot or do not distinguish between business *transactions* and the *acquisition* of new business and new relationships.   In the case of networking, it's **not about the transaction**.

The 9 to 5 Networker may not want to "do business" with family members or friends and that's a choice that comes from their own value system. The problem with 9 to 5 Networkers is that they never leverage the power of their other networks. They are as myopic in their viewing of family members as "just family members." They tend to view friends just as people with similar interests, with whom they share great times and have a great camaraderie.

What they fail to realize is that every family member and every friend belongs to multiple networks, many of which the 9 to 5 Networker *does not* belong. For example, your spouse or partner has a network they belong to at their job; they also may coach or belong to a sports team or to a parents' group. Maybe they are members at a certain gym that you don't belong to, or shop in certain neighborhood stores that you don't. They may know different people than you, perhaps others who they came into contact with while attending school, or who are friends of friends through social networking sites.

9 to 5 Networkers are a bit ironic and can get hysterical at times. While they typically do not view their friends and family as referral sources or as people who could help them to meet new business contacts, they tend to get angry when they realized an opportunity has passed them by. This usually happens when a friend or family member shares a story about another person that they know who needed or used the products or services that the 9 to 5 Networker offers, but the person did not get those products or services from the 9 to 5 Networker

A very common reaction is hearing them say, "Why didn't you tell them that I could help? Why didn't you think of me?" More often than not, it's the 9 to 5 Networkers fault, not the other person's fault for failing to recognize the opportunity and to know how to take action. This is because the 9 to 5 Networker didn't train others to help spot the opportunity in the first place.

My Cousin Eddie:

In 1999, I was attending a family reunion at which my third-cousin, Albina was also in attendance. She was 70 year old, and was really happy to see me as we had not seen each other in several years. With pride, she told me that her son, (my second-cousin) Eddie, had graduated from law school, had passed the bar examination and was now a lawyer at a very prestigious law firm in New York City.

At that time, Eddie was 51 and was always somewhat (and still is) an enigma in our family. We knew he had multiple degrees from a variety of Ivy League and other prestigious colleges and universities. He could read, write and speak several languages fluently. He was able to converse on almost any subject with ease and with great knowledge. Yet for years, *no one in the family knew what he did – including his mother!* We used to joke around that he was a secret agent for the government.

"So what kind of law is he practicing?" I asked.

"Well....law, The American kind," she replied.

"Ok, but what area of specialization? Bankruptcy? Criminal? Real Estate? Personal Injury?" I inquired.

"You know, I don't really know, but I know he's a great lawyer, or at least he'd better be with all the money spent on his schooling," she seriously said.

"Do you have his business card?" I asked.

"Actually I don't have one with me, he never gave me one. He just told me to have anyone with a legal problem give him a call. I'll give you his home number and you can talk to him," she said.

I'm sure that many people have heard parents brag about their son 'THE LAWYER' or their daughter 'THE DOCTOR' or their grandchild 'THE BUSINESS OWNER', or whatever profession they are in. But like my cousin, many of them are not familiar with what their son or daughter really does for a living. All they know is that they paid for their kid to go to medical school, law school, graduate school or they may have loaned them money to start a business. In their eyes, their child is a success.

After the conversation ended, I thought to myself about the many golden opportunities both of my cousins had missed. Albina missed the opportunity for her son to acquire new clients. It was bad enough she didn't know what type of law he practiced, but what made it even worse is that Eddie never supplied her with any of his business cards.

"You do business between 9 and 5. You build business before and after 'regular' business hours. The most powerful business in America is not conducted during business hours."
– Jeffrey Gitomer, *The Little Back Book of Connections*

How to Avoid Becoming a 9 to 5 Networker:

9 to 5 Networkers never really tell people what it is they do for a living, or they make the assumption people *really* know what they do. To avoid becoming a 9 to 5 Networker, and instead become an "Always On" Networker, your first step is to educate your immediate network – that is your family and friends – as to what you do. This doesn't mean that they need to know all of the technicalities of what you do for a living. At the very least, you need to train them to listen for key words, or to look for certain circumstances where they may be able to provide a solution to someone's problem.

For example, if you are in real estate, tell your family and friends that if they hear someone say that they are thinking of moving to a smaller home because their kids are all grown up and have left the house, that person may be a potential client for you. You may want to train your mom, dad, spouse or friends how to 1) identify a need, 2) provide a solution to the person's problem, 3) give them a call to action [tell them what they need to do] and 4) make them (your family/friends) prospect for future clients by giving out your business card, plus an extra card in case that person knows someone else who can benefit from your services.

These conversations come up all the time, especially at family gatherings and amongst friends. Out of fear, the 9 to 5 Networker will usually ignore them. But a 9 to 5 Networker who is transitioning to an "Always On" Networker will turn it into an opportunity.

A sample conversation between you (the soon-to-be "Always On" Networker) and your mom could go like this:

Mom: "My neighbor Jane was telling me now that she and George are retired, they are thinking of moving to Florida because they want to be closer to their daughter, Alyssa and their three grandchildren."

You: "Mom, I may be able to help them. Can you find out if they have already spoken to a Real Estate agent? If they have, just ask them if their agent has their Seniors Real Estate Specialist$^{®}$ designation."

Mom: "What's that?"

You: "As a Realtor$^{®}$ I have completed a course by the National Board of Realtors which gave me the necessary knowledge and expertise to counsel clients age 50+. I help them through major financial and lifestyle transitions involved in relocating, refinancing, or selling their family home. Please give them my card and tell them I would be happy to answer any questions they may have. They can call or email me anytime they want."

Mom: "I never knew that you had a specialty. I'll let Jane know.

You: "Mom, you know a lot of people who are 50+. Some

of them belong to your book club, some of them worked at your job. If you ever hear someone say they are looking to move or maybe they have a family member who needs to move, would you please tell them that you know someone who could help."

Mom: "Sure I will. By the way, how come you didn't tell me about this specialty?"

You: "Well, Mom, you never asked, and I honestly thought you wouldn't care..."

Mom: "...I'm your mother, of course I care and I shouldn't have to ask. Aww, I'm so proud of you!" she says as she gives you a big hug.

If you want to become an "Always On" Networker, instead of a 9 to 5 Networker, people need to know who you are and what you do for a living. Start by training your family members, your friends and clients to get the word out there about you. Remember, your focus in training them is on business and contact *acquisition* not the sales *transaction.* Once you do, you will start to see results and more importantly, referrals.

Section 2:
Environmental Disasters

"The name of the game is networking: businessmen meeting other businessmen for the purpose of meeting them again, at a later date."
"Networking." *The Kids In The Hall*. (1990)

Some of *The World's Worst Networkers* are indigenous to specific environments, such as a business function, a networking group, a trade show or even a social event. Just like an oil spill, a nuclear meltdown or gas leak, these types of networkers are true environmental disasters that have an economic and environmental impact on all who experience them. But unlike natural disasters, they can be prevented, if we know who they are and are able to recognize the signs.

"It's easier to prevent a mistake, than to clean up after a disaster." **– Tim Houston**

Chapter 12

Trade Show Train Wrecks

Tim Houston

Each year I participate in several business expos and trade shows representing BNI, the world's largest business networking organization. The shows we participate in are not industry specific; rather they are the types that reach a general business audience in specific geographic areas averaging between 200-300 exhibitors and close to 4,000 attendees. The vast majority of the attendees and exhibitors are small businesses or business people who are looking for ways to grow their business.

Participating in these trades shows and expos are important to us. As an organization with over 150,000 members in tens of thousands of local chapters, in 50+ countries, BNI does not advertise or market in the same manner as most "traditional business." Instead, BNI members are businesspeople that form relationships with others in non-competing businesses, by attending weekly chapter meetings and by providing qualified referrals to one another. Chapters grow primarily through the word-of-mouth invitations to attend local meetings. Our participation in trade shows and business expos help increase awareness in the business community. They also give our members an opportunity to invite people to have a first-hand experience of our system.

Trade Shows and Business Expos are considered by some

to be one of the most expensive types of networking events. A booth or table can cost a few hundred dollars for a one day event, to several thousand for a multi-day event. While this may cause some people to cringe at the mere thought of participating in a trade show, I love participating in these events as I get a chance to meet and network face-to-face with thousands of people; from those who are from well established "brick and mortar" companies, to new and innovative start-ups. Even though the costs may be exorbitant to some, it amazes me that almost without fail, at every single one of these events I will always encounter exhibitors or attendees that are among *The World's Worst Networkers*. I call them The Trade Show Train Wrecks.

Trade Show Train Wrecks are among the most ineffective, annoying types of networkers. Whether they take the form of an exhibitor or an attendee, they share similar qualities and characteristics which undoubtedly inhibit their ability to effectively network with others. In general, they do not look to build relationships at trade shows and will even exhibit similar behaviors in the real world.

Six of the most easily identifiable Trade Show Train Wrecks are:

The Dictator: This person is usually attending or exhibiting with a group of people. As an exhibitor, The Dictator will give orders to the rest of the booth's staff but will rarely help them out. They will hardly interact with people who come to visit their booth, except in cases where the Dictator overhears something being said by a staff member that they don't like. At that point they will rudely interrupt their staff person, sometimes even physically moving the person out of the way in order to take over the conversation. As an attendee, a Dictator will send their team out to try to "get business" and will position themselves in a central location, (usually close to any food or drinks), expecting their "troops" to check in every so often with updates on potential leads. Often, a Dictator will gravitate towards others from different companies, who have like-minded traits. If someone they do not know *dares* to approach them, they typically will brush them off or divert them to one of "their underlings".

The Introvert: While it is true that Introverts can be great networkers,[6] when it comes to networking at trade shows, the introvert tries to hide in the background. As an exhibitor, the Introvert will avoid as many people as possible, only talking to people on his team, silently dreading that he was told to be there. They will take frequent "bathroom breaks" or say that they have to "make a call" in order to get away to someplace in the venue where there are less people. I have seen many Introverts standing outside of the venue, "on a call" or texting someone. If forced to stay in their booth, very often they will be on their computer, silently complaining and telling themselves that they

---

[6] Misner, Ivan R., Mike Macedonio, and Mike Garrison. "To Be Good at Networking, You Have to Be a Real 'People Person'" *Truth or Delusion?: Busting Networking's Biggest Myths*. Nashville: Nelson Business, 2006. Print.

wish to be back at their job. As an attendee, the Introvert will generally walk around the show, stopping on occasion at a booth, taking some literature or promotional items. When an exhibitor attempts to talk to them, they quickly say that they were "just browsing" and quickly move on down the aisle, usually bypassing several other exhibitors until they feel safe and out of sight of the person who attempted to speak to them.

The Party Animal: These are the people who can't wait for the expo and are usually the first to volunteer to work the booth! They love to get out of town for a few days, or if the show is local, out of the office for the day. While they operate under the pretense of working, they are not there to network or to really *do work* at the show. Instead, their focus is on the receptions, lunches, dinners and cocktail parties sponsored by vendors or the organization hosting the show. The only thing they care about is having a good time, on someone else's dime. After all, they are away from their families and other responsibilities and can "let loose." As an exhibitor, they party hard into the early morning hours, only to show up the day after a reception to the work the booth; sometimes with a huge hangover, wearing dark glasses, drinking lots of coffee, avoiding as many people (and their boss) as much as they can.

As an attendee, they typically will patronize the exhibitors who are known for throwing the big parties and will purposely schmooze the staff in the hope of getting an invitation. By the way, people typically assume the Party Animal is a male, but there are a good number of female party animals as well.

The Professor: This is the person who either created the product or service, or works on the technical side of it. In general, they have little, if any, networking skills, let alone marketing or sales skills. They may have read a book or learned from someone that they must participate in trade shows in order to increase awareness about their product or service, so they exhibit. As an exhibitor, their booth will generally have a working sample of their products or prototypes of what is yet to come. Their booth will also lack the attractiveness needed to get people to come over. Some Professors can also have the Introvert's personality, while others are very outgoing. In either case, they tend to be brilliant and know the details and intricacies of their product, yet they tend to bore or lose most people in conversations (except for other Professors).

Professors also tend to have an air of superiority about themselves, usually becoming combative at the first challenge given to them by someone else in a similar business or field, or when asked a question by someone who wants a more "basic" explanation about their service or produce. As attendees, Professors typically will seek out similar products and attempt to get as much information as possible for their own research purposes, taking up very valuable time of the exhibitor's staff members. I once saw a Professor spend over an hour at a booth monopolizing the time of the booth's sole staffer and exhibiting behavior that was borderline harassment. Because he was relentless (and because the staffer was alone), many other patrons passed the booth by.

The Serial Sales Killer: Perhaps the worst of the Trade Show Train Wrecks, the Serial Sales Killer does not (or refuses to) understand that networking *is not selling!* The Serial Sales Killer fits right into Zita Gustin's (www.thesavvynetworker.com) explanation of why some people confuse networking with selling:

> "Please understand that most [of these] folks just don't know better. They THINK that business networking is all about selling AND they operate from a "now money now" approach, wherein their goal is to leave the event with a certain amount of appointments booked, contracts signed, or a bill of sale in their hands. These folks are seen as pushy and aggressive and this selling approach leaves a wide wake of missed opportunities behind them[7]."

Serial Sales Killers believe that *everyone* they meet is a potential victim (customer) and will attempt to sell their product or service. Within seconds of meeting their victim, a Serial Sales Killer will launch into their sales pitch with an expectation that

---

[7]   *The #1 Myth About Networking*. Dir. Zita Gustin. Perf. Zita Gustin. *The Savvy Networker - Networking That Sticks!* Web. 1 Nov. 2010. <http://www.thesavvynetworker.com/videotips.html>.

the other person will buy from them. They talk and talk and talk, and rarely -- if ever – listen to what the other person says. They view the trade show or expo as a placc to show off their closing techniques or use it as a venue to practice on others for much "bigger and better" targets outside of the show.

How to Avoid a Train Wreck:

Whether you are an exhibitor or an attendee at an expo or trade show, have specific goals in mind and do everything you can to achieve them. But be aware there is a great chance several Trade Show Train Wrecks will be in attendance. While it may be difficult to avoid them, the easiest thing you can do is to be prepared for them.

When you encounter one of them, keep in mind that no matter how bad the Train Wreck is, you are representing your business and other people will notice how you react. Maintain your dedication, integrity, commitment, professionalism. Be engaging and do your best to steer clear or to minimize your time and interaction with the Train Wrecks. Just like passing a car accident on a highway, Trade Show Train Wrecks will slow you down and if you're not careful or aware, you too could end up a victim in a pile-up.

Chapter 13

Business Networking Thieves

Jason Cobine

You were a new networker once. I know when I was, I made more mistakes than most. You've probably learned valuable tips from others that were more experienced. Here's an example of how you can spot a networking theft; why someone else's networking "crime" may affect you and discover how you can help rehabilitate them.

Imagine meeting someone when you are networking who doesn't know who they want to meet or who they can introduce you to. They might try and sell directly to you or say they want to meet anybody, somebody or everybody (pick from "that wants a cheaper mortgage" or "that needs to increase their income" or "that would like to grow their business"). You probably want to help them yet you can't because your contact book is not divided into anybody's, somebody's or everybody's. How many times a week do people tell you they need to increase their income? I'm sure it's not many, yet this is something that most people want. It may be considered intrusive to ask such a direct question.

Do frustrated networkers need to be more specific?

If a networker gets frustrated when you try and ask them to be specific it may be because they think that their service is required by most people they meet. They might even be right – a lot of people want all three of the above. But you might not be networking to look for services or you may have only just commenced a contract with people that do what they do. You don't have time to ask everyone you meet if they want the things mentioned at events.

This kind of frustration occurs quite often at large networking events because there are lots of people starting their networking journey – we all started somewhere so it's forgivable – this isn't the theft, it's more of an innocent mistake. Perhaps naughty if repeated by an experienced networker.

Are businesses networking groups being targeted?

The moral theft is usually committed around a table where the only weapons might be a knife and fork or awful coffee. Imagine a business networking group where everyone has paid a membership fee and agreed that they're committed to helping others in the group generate more business and are happy to accept introductions in return. If you've ever been to one of these groups you've probably witnessed a networking theft, yet you might not realize what's happening because it's not immediately obvious.

What are networkers doing that is so wrong? If they're not preparing for the event and not asking for introductions to specific people they can only be hurting themselves, right? Wrong!

If they're asking to be introduced to anybody, somebody or everybody surely the only person to suffer from a lack of quality introductions is themselves? Absolutely wrong! It is so wrong it should be classed as a networking crime!

How does this affect my business networking groups?

There are people in business networking groups taking up space that could be used by someone that prepares properly and knows what they're looking for. If they had prepared they could spend time listening to the requests from the rest of the group. The guilty will not see themselves as naughty networkers and the usual remedy is to leave them to their own devices. Does that help anyone? I don't think it does as members will leave if they are not receiving what they ask for.

Here are three reasons why this will end up affecting the individual members and the group as a whole.

1: Networking thieves are **not listening** to others that are asking for help because they're too busy thinking about what they're going to say. If networkers don't listen, how can they keep their promise to help others? Imagine if no-one in a group heard what anyone else asked for. The group would lack introductions.

2: They may also be **blocking well connected business** people from joining the group because they are "competition". They don't realize that the "competition" are able to bring everyone qualified leads. The "competition" might get asked for your service all the time yet they have no-one they know well enough to introduce.

3: Some networkers only joined a group on the condition that they could take two places, which is fine when they bring the amount of referrals two people would. But what if they don't? **The referral count isn't as high as it could be**. I'm not saying that they are not nice people – but should they really have made a commitment they have no intention of keeping?

How to spot a Networking Thief:

There are good indicators; no pen, no notepaper yet plenty of cards, oh yes, hundreds of the little devils.

How do you avoid meeting one? You probably can't yet you can help rehabilitate them by asking them what sort of introductions they want, then explaining that you are unlikely to find any for them if they are not specific. Give them an example of how asking for something specific worked for you. They may even thank you for helping them out. If you meet them at one of your groups and they have more than one "hot seat" you can also encourage them to allow someone else to take one of their places. This can be achieved if you ask them to help choose the right person.

How to stop a Networking Thief:

Not everyone "gets it" straight away so lead by example – prepare and ask for someone or something specific when the opportunity arises, you'll be amazed what happens. When others see how successful you are at generating qualified introductions for yourself they might ask how you do it. That's when you get the opportunity to help others by suggesting they do the same.

Chapter 14

The Cheerleader And The Spectator

Tim Houston

It has been said that networking, in all its forms, is a "contact sport." Whether it's business networking, online networking, or face-to-face social networking, when playing this "game" the goal is to form new relationships or enhance existing ones, resulting in the sharing and/or introduction of new contacts with the other players.

Often at a networking "game" (i.e. event, venue or networking group), there are many players; but often hidden amongst the players, there are some who pose as team players. These are two of *The World's Worst Networkers*: The Cheerleader and The Spectator.

Go Team! Go!

The Cheerleader is usually a person who stands on the sidelines and looks good – *really good* – to the casual observer and is often mistaken as a player. Cheerleaders often have a vibrant personality which leaves a really good impression with most people that they meet. They are well-mannered, professional and in general, very outgoing.

At face-to-face events, they arrive early to support the organization and the networking players. On Social Networking sites like Facebook, they tend to "like" everything you do and put a lot of positive comments in response to *anything* you post. You could say that you just bought a roll of paper towels and they'll *like* it. You can count on them to physically or virtually be there, no matter what.

So far it sounds good, doesn't it? Who wouldn't want a person like this in their network? Every team and player needs to be motivated to keep up the morale, right?

Sure, that's great and appears to work – until you or your network needs the Cheerleader to do more than cheer – you need them to work the network or help to build it by having them in the game as a player introducing you to new people or providing referrals.

In order to keep up appearances, they will often react by referring themselves as a potential client to people on your team, whether or not they need the products or services of those people. When someone asks for an introduction to a potential new client or source of referrals, a Cheerleader will often ask a family member or a friend to "do them a favor" to listen or meet with the networker, or visit the networking group, even if they don't have an interest.

When it is time to give an endorsement or testimonial, more often than not, all a Cheerleader can do is to provide a laundry list of "thank yous" to people on the team, ("I want to thank John the accountant for preparing my taxes; Thanks to Daisy, the florist, for providing me with beautiful flowers; Dr. Jones, the chiropractor for adjusting my spine, etc.).

Sometimes when under pressure, a Cheerleader might respond to a request by saying, "I support the team in other ways, doesn't that matter?" While you do recognize and value their support, they need to know that in order to be a part of the team, they need to be an active player and can't sit on the sidelines.

The Spectator

Unlike the Cheerleader, the Spectator watches the game from afar, usually criticizing every move made by the players and their coaches.

The Spectator is an interesting person. When they get "involved" in building a networking group or team, the Spectator will do the minimal amount of work necessary, if any. Their actions prove that they do not really want be a player – but they want to earn just as much as a player. They often refuse or make excuses why they cannot reach into their outside networks to invite other people to get involved with their new networking team. They complain that they barely have time to attend the weekly "game" and they don't want to be involved in the practice – that is the necessary education and tasks in putting together a team. They think they can learn the rules of the games based upon their observation, but never through actual training, studying and practice.

Sometimes out of a sense of desperation, a team will keep a spectator. If the team is winning – that is if the networking team is generating referrals, having large sums of closed business and growing with new members – a spectator feels like they're winning too. This is because the Spectator believes that through his association with the team, people in his world will view him as a "mover and shaker." Like fans of professional sports, Spectators will go out and brag how "their team" is doing so well, although in networking, they will often position themselves in their stories as one of the star players. In reality they're often "up in the stands" watching the game happen.

When the team isn't progressing ahead, Spectators will do nothing more than provide an avalanche of comments and critiques. They will whine and moan about how bad the team is, how the players and coaches don't care and how the game isn't worth playing because "networking doesn't really work". Usually, in these situations, Spectators will not offer any solution-focused ideas; they will instead lambaste and lament to anyone who will listen to them.

> *"[I]ndividual commitment to a group effort - that is what makes a team work, a company work, a society work, a civilization work".*
> --Vince Lombardi

THE LESSON: Successful networking is dependent upon players who are committed to the team, not the Spectators or Cheerleaders. Cheerleaders may be good for morale and are nice to watch, but they offer nothing else in terms of team performance and earnings.[8] Spectators pay to see the networking game, spending large sums of money and time, yet often never seeing a return other than the bragging rights when the team does well or criticism when it's not.

While both the Spectator and the Cheerleader do have their places in professional sports, in the game of networking they need to do more than just be there – they have to transition into players and they need to *play the game!*

Just as in professional sports, even the average networking player makes more money.[9] From the outset, whenever you meet or discover a Cheerleader or Spectator in your ranks, you need to be up-front and explain why you need players, and why you need them to contribute on the field. If they agree and transition from Cheerleader or Spectator to a player, you are off to having a successful season. If they don't, or if they refuse, it is best to send them packing and on their way.

---

[8] In 2010, the salary for a Dallas Cowboy Cheerleader – the most famous professional Cheerleaders in the world – is $50 per game and they don't get paid to attend the 2 to 5 rehearsals, *per week!* All of the requirements are found at the Dallas Cowboys Cheerleader's Official Webpage at http://www.dallascowboyscheerleaders.com/auditions/auditions_rules.cfm

[9] According to USA Today, In 2009, average salary of an NFL football player was $770,000.00 and in 2010, the average salary of a professional Major League Baseball player was over $1.5 Million. See "USATODAY.com Salaries Database." *USAToday.com*. Web. 01 Nov. 2010. <http://content.usatoday.com/sports/football/nfl/salaries/mediansalaries.aspx?year=2009> and <http://content.usatoday.com/sports/baseball/salaries/mediansalaries.aspx?year=2010>

Chapter 15

Silly Sarah And Jack The Jerk

Robyn Henderson

SILLY SARAH:

I was speaking in Sydney at a business networking event at one of the 5 star hotels. The client was a stickler for details and was expecting 250 guests at the breakfast presentation. Her plan was to open the doors at 7:20 AM, have the staff start serving the hot plated breakfast at 7:30 AM and I would start speaking at 7:40 AM, continuing through to 8:40 AM – she wanted to make sure that they got value for their money – even though I thought they were very optimistic that 250 people would be served in less than 10 minutes – let alone be seated in 10 minutes!

That day, I was wearing a navy suit and white shirt and as planned the doors opened at 7:20 AM. To speed up the process, I decided to assist in welcoming people to the event and direct them to their corporate tables or encourage them to join tables where there was free seating.

At around 7:27 AM, a woman wearing a bright red jacket/suit approached me – "Hi, I am Robyn thanks for joining us this morning, are you meeting friends here?' I said.

"Yes I am with the Acorn Company" she said

"Just head towards the front of the room, their table is located just to the left of the podium." I said.

"Get me a pen and paper, I've heard this woman is quite

good!" she demanded.

"Sure will" I said. Making my way to Jean, one of the wait staff I had previously befriended, and who was also dressed in a navy uniform and white shirt, I said – "Excuse me Jean, I wonder if you can help me. Do you see that lady, wearing a red jacket and sitting on the front table – would you be able to take her a pen and writing pad and when you give it to her, just point to me – so she knows where it has come from?"

"Certainly Robyn, no problem"

7:45 AM (only slightly behind schedule): my client welcomed everyone to the event and read my introduction. As I walked to the podium, in my navy suit and white shirt, I passed the dragon in the red jacket and smiled at her. Her mouth gaped, her face reddened and she looked decidedly guilty – and as she was less than 2 meters from the stage she squirmed for my entire presentation.

One of the points I made during my presentation was that no one is a nobody. Everyone has at least one influential network that they have access to or play a major part in – whether it is work related, cultural, special interest – everyone is a sphere of influence in at least one network. The challenge of course is that no one wears a sign saying be really nice to me – I am going to introduce you to your next biggest client, next best friend, next partner – you just take people at face value and try not to judge people – everyone has merit, everyone has value.

After the presentation, I was signing books and chatting to

the guests. The lady in the red jacket was hanging around waiting to speak to me, when the crowd had thinned.

"Robyn, my name is Sarah, I owe you an apology – I thought you were the waitress – I am so sorry."

"Thank you Sarah, but you don't owe me an apology. I actually think you owe the wait staff the apology. Have you ever taken the time to get to know any of these staff? The bulk of them are university students, who work the breakfast shift and then head to university classes for the day. Most are qualified professionals in their own country and have moved to Australia and their qualifications are not recognized in Australia, and they can't get work – so they take whatever work they can get – including waitressing. Sarah, always remember that no one is a nobody."

"Okay, I get it. What books do you think I need?" she asked. I replied, "Sarah, I think you need the full set, plus the DVDs." Sarah made her purchases and left the room. What I had not realized was that some of the waitresses had heard my conversation as they were clearing the tables nearby.

"Robyn, thank you for what you said to that lady. So many people ignore us and treat us like we are invisible, thanks for standing up for us."

"Anytime ladies, you do a great job"

Did Sarah learn her message? I may never know, but I'm sure she read the books.

JACK THE JERK

I was attending a business after hours event at a beach side function center and noticed when I arrived that there was a narrow entrance to the function room where the registration table was located and quite a backlog of people trying to enter the room. As I joined the queue, I made a mental note to give the organizers a few tips post event about how to create better registration system and smoother processing – purely by locating the registration at a different entrance to the large room.

Once in the room, I made my way to the back of the room, where I not only got a better view of who was in the room, but also had room to breathe.

One of my networking strategies is to act like the host and not the guest. I noticed a young girl about 21/22 years of age, nervously standing all alone.

"Hi I am Robyn, do you mind if I join you?"

"Thank you so much, my name is Jane and I am absolutely terrified – my boss sent me here to network and I have no idea what I am doing and I am going to be in serious trouble if I don't get some business here tonight – and I might lose my job" she babbled.

"Slow down breathe you are going to be fine. I write books about networking and you are going to have a really fun night – just stick with me and I will show you what to do."

"Thanks so much, I feel better already," replied Jane.

Little did we know the night had a long way to go. As we

were chatting away and getting to know a little about each other, out of the corner of my eye, I noticed a well-dressed middle aged man approaching us. He seemed to be a man with a mission and was blunt to say the least.

"Where are you from?' he asked

"Hi, my name is Robyn, what's yours?" I asked

"Jack. Where are you from? He mumbled. I could have been smart and given the location I had come from – but I knew he wanted my business name.

"Networking To Win is my company – I write books about networking and business building."

"Hmmph! You?" nodding towards Jane, who had reverted back to a nervous stuttering mess.

"My, my name's Jane – I work with XYZ (one of the largest financial groups in Australia).

"Mmm- give me your card." said Jack.

"And Jack what business are you in?" I asked

"Procurement." He said very vaguely.

"Do you have a business card Jack?" I asked

"NO! – Card Jane!" he demanded.

I gently put my hand on Jane's hand as she was digging in her bag for her business card and shook my head. "Sorry Jack, Jane forgot her cards tonight and we've just seen our friend, so we'll leave you to it Jack – enjoy your night."

As we walked away, Jane said – "Robyn, you were quite rude to Jack."

"Jane, are you kidding me. Jack, in my opinion, is a cowboy – he is rude, belligerent and made no attempt to even start a conversation – he was purely here to collect business cards and offend people. And had you given him your business card, he would be on the phone first thing tomorrow demanding to sell whatever he sells to you. **Jane: lesson number one – when you value you, other people value you too. And <u>never</u> <u>*ever*</u> accept rudeness at a networking event.** If someone can't be civil to you, you really don't want them to do business with you.

My golden rule of networking at business events is DON'T SELL. Just connect, get to know the other person and take the first step in building that bridge of trust. This may or may not result in business – but you will be remembered for all the right reasons. Let's talk to this guy over here, he looks a bit lost. "

"Hi, I'm Robyn, this is Jane, mind if we join you?"

"Sure, I'm Roger."

Believe it or not, Roger ended up having a great time with the two of us. This was not his normal network; he was filling in for his boss and felt a bit lost. However, once we got to know each other (through conversations not about work, but about what we did outside of work) Roger ended up being a great connection for Jane – and once he found out what she was after - actually invited her to another event the next night that he was hosting – and she made some great connections, who ultimately became clients soon after.

And Roger did end up knowing quite a few people at the event and he was very generous with his introductions for both Jane and me.

The morning after the first event Jane phoned me to thank me for befriending her and let me know her boss was singing her praises to all her team that morning. He was still dumbfounded as to how she got invited to Roger's event that evening. Her response – "Networking boss, networking!"

We laughed about Jack, the rude cowboy, who no doubt would continue to attend networking events, not realizing it was not about selling it was all about connecting. I ran into Jane at many events over the next few months, and whenever we do, we always have a laugh about Jack The Jerk!

Chapter 16

The Over-Involved Networker

Tim Houston

There are people who belong to *too many* things.

Steven owned an advertising company for over 25 years. He was a very successful, well-known businessman that was very active in a variety of business, service and fraternal organizations, both on a local and regional level. Steven was very proud to have served in many leadership positions and he did little to keep this a secret, making sure to tell everyone.

When I met Steven, he was currently serving as a Scout Master in the Boy Scouts; he was a member of the Board of Directors of the local chapter of a major charitable organization; he was very active in his local church and had served on its community council as its President; he also belonged to a local Rotary International chapter and had been the recipient of the Paul Harris Fellow Award. A few months before we met, he had just finished his final term serving as the Vice President of the Homeowners' Association in the community where he lived. Steven's past also included being the President of the local Chamber of Commerce and at one time, was also very involved in local politics, serving as an elected official.

There was no doubt that Steven had strong relationships with many people in the community. When he found out about a local networking group, he visited, and loved it so much that he

applied for membership right on the spot. The chapter's
Membership Committee interviewed Steven and checked his
references, which were stellar. A week later, Steven was being
inducted as its newest member.

Right from the start, Steven was a great member,
contributing referrals and inviting visitors to his chapter. He
made it a point to have individual meetings with the members.
By all accounts, no one was surprised that in less than six months,
Steven was nominated and agreed to serve in a leadership position
in his group as its newest President. He attended training and
seemed to grasp the organization's principles, policies, guidelines,
traditions and Code of Ethics.

About three weeks into his tenure as President, things
started to change. Steven believed that his networking group's
breakfast meetings should start just like his church's Community
Council meetings: with a prayer of grace before eating the meal.
He also decided that the meeting would start by having everyone
stand up while leading his group in reciting a positive affirmation
of his choice for that week. Some people in the group first
thought it wasn't a big deal; after all it was common at events
such as government meetings and in university graduations and
award celebrations to have someone recite a generic prayer as part
of an invocation. They also thought that the positive affirmation
would help "fire up" the group. Others, however, called me to
complain.

The veteran members immediately notice a drastic

change. Little by little, Steven would introduce things that *he* liked from the other organizations and groups that he belonged to; he thought if it worked well in those groups, it would also work well in his networking group. Within a month's time, people were having a completely different experience and the group bore little resemblance to what it was supposed to be.

Most people in the group feared to speak out against Steven because of how well-connected and how well-known he was in the business community. They thought if they challenged him, they would face some sort of retribution in these outside groups. Steven also gave a lot of referrals to his members and some thought if they addressed him, it would be like biting the hand that fed them. Instead, many took the position of "grin and bear it," secretly hoping that things would change on their own, or that I would take action against Steven. To those that contacted me, I promised them I would address these issues the following week when I visited.

When I did visit the group in my role as its Director, I was astonished by what I saw upon walking into the room. Steven had made a big sign which announced the name of the group. Normally this wouldn't be a problem but it became an issue when he decided to change the color of the organization's trademarked logo. I questioned Steven as to why this was done and he readily told me that as an *experienced advertising agency owner,* he knew what colors would work best to attract new members. Besides, in his opinion, the organization's color was *"boring"* and was *"so*

1980's." When I pointed out that he could not do this due to trademarks and copyrights and other legal reasons, he reluctantly took the sign down. I thought that would be the end of the Steven's changes, but instead, it got worse.

The open networking part of the meeting seemed to last longer than it should have. Steven started the meeting 15 minutes later than it was supposed to because he had walked out of the room to take a phone call from an *important client.* Because of his tardiness, he told his group that they would skip over the affirmation and prayer for the day and get right down to introductions to get back on track. He told each of the 30 members of the group that they had 15 seconds to deliver their introductions and he would bang a gavel (which he brought) when they exceeded their time.

After the second time that Steven ferociously banged the gavel with such force that it sounded like a construction project, people kept to the time limit, speaking faster than an auctioneer. At this particular meeting, there were two guests attending. Steven told them that instead of giving them an opportunity to introduce themselves after the members, "in the interest of time" they could talk to members after the meeting.

The rest of the meeting continued without a hitch, following the proper format. Steven actually became very pleasant. I thought it was too good to be true – and it was.

At the end of the meeting, Steven announced to the group that during the week an application was submitted by Miguel, a local florist who I thought I had seen at the start of the meeting and who was no longer there. Steven then proceeded to read Miguel's application to the entire group and asked the members to vote on the application. This is where I had to jump in and stop him dead in his tracks, explaining to Steven that this was not the way our organization did things. The chapter has a Membership Committee who dealt with these matters and that he, as President, had nothing to do with it.

In reply Steven had the audacity to tell me that *I* was out of order and that it should be done this way; after all, this was how his fraternal organization's lodge did it and they had over 200 members and had been formed way before I was even born!

I explained to Steven that what he did in his other organizations was different than what we did, and that he was trying to transform his chapter into something that it was not supposed to be. I used the analogy that you don't show up to play baseball with a basketball and a hockey mask. There were rules and procedures to follow in any business. I privately told Steven that if he decided not to follow the proper, approved format, we would have no choice but to relieve him of his position. He didn't take this very well and told me "we'll see about that."

A week or two later, I received a phone call from a member saying that she was quitting the group as Steven decided that the following week's meeting was going to be a "businessmen's only meeting." The women members of the chapter would be able to attend the week after and in a month's time, as Steven put it, "the girls could have their own meeting." Before 3 pm that day, six others threatened to resign (four of which were men) unless something was done to stop Steven.

At 6 pm that night, after a dozen email messages and phone calls, I connected with Steven and confronted him, asking why he did this. He told me that he believed that the men of the group should have a meeting once every other month to help them to bond easier and to be free to talk without having to be worried about "offending any of the *babes* in the group." After all, there were organizations like the Boy Scouts and Girl Scouts and there were private associations for women and minorities only. I reminded him that he was outright discriminating against people because our organization wasn't like that, at which point I relieved him of his duties as President. At that moment, Steven decided that he didn't want to be a part of any organization that wouldn't have him as a member. He resigned right after he threatened to sue me and our organization for "defamation of his character and business interference." As someone who had worked in the legal profession for many years, this didn't scare me one bit.

The saga of Steven did not end there.

At next week's meeting, Steven showed up, announced to everyone that *he was leaving* and that he was starting his own networking group, apart from ours. He berated me and the organization for not being "creative enough" and for being "stuck in the past." Steven told the member that they should come to his networking group which would be held next week, at the same restaurant, but on the other side, at the same time as this chapter's meeting. After all, there would be no mandatory meetings, no "childish rules" and no fees to pay, except for meals.

Only one person took Steven up on his offer: a client of his that he sponsored into the chapter. Steven's networking group never got off the ground, while the group he was formerly a member of, flourished.

Word-of-mouth travels fast. What is talked about in one meeting at 7:00 am can spread like a wild-fire to hundreds of others, before noon. This was the case with Steven. People heard from others how he treated people, and how he wanted to be the master of his own domain. This eventually had an ugly effect on his business.

As time went by, I learned that Steven's behavior in our organization was just as bad – if not worse – in many of the other organizations he belong to. Eventually, those other groups removed him from leadership positions or ousted him as a member. His business eventually closed, though I heard, through word-of-mouth, that he retired and sold it to a competitor.

There are people who can become over-involved in many organizations. While it is important in terms of business development and networking to belong to more than one network, you need to respect the rules, policies and procedures of each individual organization. Steven's inability to separate these, and his attempts to pick-and-choose the rules that suited him, ended up costing him relationships, his reputation and his business.

Chapter 17

May THIS Force NOT Be With You!
Michelle R. Donovan

As we grow up into adulthood, we learn that we are surrounded by invisible forces. For example, the force of gravity - where would we be without it ... literally? The force of magnetism ... how would MRI machines work without it? The force of nature ... it surrounds us with its glory and impressive strength, in every corner of the planet. The force of friction ... it produces kilowatts of energy for our society. And how could we forget the galactic force of good ... "may the force be with you"!

However, as many of us chose to enter into the business world, no one directly taught us how to network effectively. No one taught us about a volatile force of networking, the force of repulsion that could take us to the brink of word of mouth disaster. The good thing is, unlike many of our natural forces, you actually can control this powerful force of networking.

The first step is becoming aware of it. The second step is adapting your behavior for the outcome you desire.

The Force of Repulsion

This force of networking will most likely bring you misery. It will repel people from you immediately. It's like an invisible barrier between you and the other person (kind of like the invisible wall between Indiana Jones and the cobra, if you saw the movie). Many times, we are left clueless as to why people walk away from us, never return our calls, or avoid eye contact with us at the table. The force of repulsion will often cause you to feel like you've wasted your time or leave you holding up the bar alone.

Let's take a look at three common behaviors often seen at networking events that initiate the force of repulsion, frequently used by some of the worst networkers in the world:

Passing out a business card to anyone and everyone in the room, like some super-hero able to leap tables in a single bound. What makes you think that everyone in the room actually wants your card? People who don't want your card will feel like you're directly selling to them and that will put up the invisible wall faster than a speeding bullet! What's your reaction to a cold call during your favorite TV show? If you're like me, you hang up before the person speaks or maybe you don't even pick up the phone. The force of repulsion is in high gear! Believe it or not, when you force your card onto anyone with a face, you might as well be cold calling ... but doing it in person.

Looking past the person you're speaking to in order to see who else is in the room. The message is clear ... this person is not interesting and you'd rather be talking to someone else at that moment. This person can read your body language very easily and who would want to hang around with someone who has better things to do or would rather be with someone else? I can think of a few marriages that ended that way! Networking is supposed to be about developing relationships. You're meeting people and trying to decide if they are people you want to get to know. It reminds me of dating. If you were on a first date and the other person kept looking around to see who was more interesting, I'll bet you wouldn't go out of your way for a second date. Why would someone in a networking event go out of their way to re-connect with you if you make they feel like a stone pillar standing between you and where you really want to be?

Talking all about YOU! There's a country song by Toby Keith that addresses this very thing in a dating situation. Have you ever been with someone who talks, talks, talks all about them? Sometimes, they don't even take a breath. I call this "verbal throw-up" … now you have an image to lock in your brain. The next time you feel yourself about to upchuck at a networking event, take a breath and ask some open ended questions. Allow the other person to speak twice as long as you. Demonstrate that you care about what they have to say. Ask them questions that will help you determine if they would be a good person to add to your network. After all, networking is all about them ... not you!

Most of us want people to like us. We want people to talk to us at networking events. Contrary to what you may have heard, networking is not a direct sales activity. It's not about closing deals and landing your biggest client. Networking is about developing relationships from the ground up. Relationships are between people. People typically don't like to be sold to, don't like to be over-looked and certainly don't like other people throwing up on them.

From this point on, you can consider yourself informed, educated and aware of one volatile, invisible force of networking. If you are guilty of any of these actions, consider modifying your behaviors accordingly. If you're not sure, ask your best friend to observe you the next time your networking. Honest feedback is the foundation of personal growth.

Chapter 18

Miserablism

Tim Houston

Several years ago, I attended a meeting of a networking group and was introduced to a relatively newer member who I will call Bill. Prior to meeting him, I was told by one of the members that Bill designed and built custom kitchens and that his work was incredible.

When I walked into the room, I noticed that he had a portfolio of his work out on a table and stopped to look at it. His work was so amazing and worthy of high praise that it should have been featured in home improvement magazines and on home design TV shows.

However, our introduction left me with a lasting, negative impression. It went something like this:

Tim: "Good morning! It's nice to meet you. How are you today?"

Bill: "Yeah, yeah, what's so good about it? Would you really want to know how I'm feeling?"

Tim: "Well it's a great day outside, the weather is beautiful and you're alive!"

Bill: "But there are others who didn't get up. There's a war going on, my property taxes just went up, my car broke down yesterday and this morning's coffee was cold... "

...and he continued to lament about the world's and his problems and issues. To say that this was one of the more interesting introductions I've had in quite some time would be an understatement.

After I diplomatically removed myself from speaking to him, I thought the following: 1) perhaps this is just a bad day for him; 2) this guy may need a referral to a psychotherapist and I could help; 3) he is a real jerk and his attitude really sucks.

When the meeting ended, I asked the person who introduced me to him if this was just an isolated event and she confided, "He's like this every week since he's been a member."

"Why would you accept someone with such a negative attitude?" I asked.

"Well he was the only custom kitchen maker that ever came and we *needed* him. It's not like we have a bunch of them knocking down our door." she said.

Attitude plays such an important role in networking. We all know people we *love* to do business with. These folks are the kind that whether we are buying from them or selling to them, we have a positive experience. We walk away without any remorse and we actually look forward to dealing with them time and again. We secretly wish that more people we deal with could be like them. Their mere presence is felt and affects everyone around them in a positive way.

Conversely, there are people that we sometimes do business with because we feel we *have* to or we believe we have no other choices. Unfortunately they often make the situation more difficult than it has to be to the point where everyone is miserable. We approach them as one might approach going to the dentist for a root-canal: it's not going to be pleasant but it "has to be done."

A few months later when it became very clear to Bill that he wasn't getting referrals, he left the group. I happened to be present at this meeting when they announced that Bill's classification was opened and without any exaggeration, there was a collective sigh of relief.

It was highly improbable that Bill or the group would have any form of mutual achievement based upon attitude alone. Bill's miserable attitude presented a barrier to his networking partners. He made it impossible for them to get to know him outside of what he projected, and thus there was absolutely no foundation for trust. Not only was Bill miserable but could you imagine the sense of misery he projected to those around him. Given these circumstances, why would anyone want to give him referrals, let alone be in the same room as him? The worst part of it all was that it seemed Bill actually *liked* being miserable.

> *"Attitudes are contagious. Is yours worth catching?"*
> — **Unknown**

Bill wasn't the only one that had a problem: the group also had an issue in that they had an attitude of desperation. By accepting Bill as the "only one" and in falsely believing that they "needed him," it gave some of the members and their guests an overall negative impression of the group as a whole.

Upon closer inspection, while they were a group that had 30-35 members, they took just anyone in as a member. They refused to qualify their candidates or to wait for someone who would be a better fit for their group. Bill's attitude was just one symptom of the group's larger problems. Because they accepted anyone as a member, there were several others who did attend the meetings but did not make any sort of a positive contribution and who also had negative, miserable attitudes.

This set the stage for disaster. Cliques had formed and there were people who did not want to deal with others who weren't in their clique. The fact that cliques formed in the first place was a tell-tale sign that there were problems not being addressed. Upon experiencing this group for the first time, many people were so turned off by the group's behavior, they decided not to participate.

While there was a room full of people, their overall attitude shined through and hindered any productivity or progress.

In the end, because members would not refer business to each other, it turned into more of a weekly social event for a few people, and the group ultimately fell apart and closed after 7 years.

> **"You get treated in life the way you teach people to treat you"**
> **– Dr. Wayne Dwyer**

Smart business people know that their attitude plays a huge role in their networking success, whether it is from the perspective of the individual networker or from the perspective of a group and organization. I believe that you do have a choice, especially when it comes to networking. Bill and his group were both self-fulfilling prophecies. As my friend, motivational speaker, author and trainer, Josh Hinds (www.getmotivation.com) says:

> "I think there's a lot of truth to the term self-fulfilling prophecy. Meaning that if a person runs around thinking of all the reasons things can't possibly work out for them, they end up giving power to the very things they don't want to have happen. In summary, we tend to get what we most focus on. That being the case, doesn't it stand to reason we would benefit from seeing things through a more optimistic lens?" [10]

---

[10] Hinds, Josh. "Josh Hinds' Motivational & Inspirational Journal." *Motivation*

Ask yourself: why would you want to do business with or be associated with someone that is consistently negative or miserable?   To others, it reflects poorly upon you and will have a negative effect on you and your business.

Whenever you find yourself having a poor or negative attitude, stop and refocus yourself on your behavior and thoughts to see exactly what you're doing. Ask yourself: how **WILL** my attitude affect me, those around me and my business? How **IS** it affecting me personally, and the relationships I have with others, right **NOW**?

Point. Motivation Advice for Your Achievement and Success. 07 July 2006. Web. 08 Sept. 2010. <http://www.getmotivation.com/2006/07/do-you-see-positive-side-of-things-by.html>.

Chapter 19

Premature Solicitation
Ivan Misner, Ph.D.

Have you ever been solicited for a referral or for business by someone you didn't even know? Michelle Villalobos, a BNI member in Miami, calls this *"Premature Solicitation."* [Say that fast three times and you might get in trouble!]

I agree completely with Michelle, and I've been a victim of "premature solicitation" many times. I was recently speaking at a business networking event and, before my presentation, someone literally came up to me and said, "Hi, it is a real pleasure to meet you. I understand you know Richard Branson. I offer specialized marketing services and I am sure his Virgin enterprises could benefit from what I provide. Could you please introduce me to him so that I can show him how this would assist his companies?"

OK, so what I was thinking was:

"Are you completely insane? I'm going to introduce you, someone I don't know and don't have any relationship with, to Sir Richard, whom I've only met a few times, so that you can proceed to attempt to sell him a product or service that I don't know anything about and haven't used myself? Yeah, right. That's NEVER going to happen."

I am pleased to report, however, that with much effort, I was able to keep that little monologue inside my own head, opting instead for a much more subtle response.

I replied... "Hi, I'm Ivan, I'm sorry–I don't think we've met before, what was your name again? " That surprised the man enough to make him realize that his "solicitation" might have been a bit "premature." I explained that I regularly refer people to my contacts, but only after I've established a long-term strong relationship with the service provider first. He said thanks and moved on to his next victim.

I shared this story in my blog and in a couple of venues, including one of my favorite online social networks. A great dialog ensued with most people sharing their horror stories and frustrations about people who pounce on them at networking meetings asking for business even though they've never met the person before.

Every time I start to think this is an almost universal feeling of distaste for that approach to networking, I am brought back to reality by the minority of people who still think that this is actually a good networking technique. To my astonishment, someone on the forum actually wrote:

> "I don't happen to believe that you need a relationship
> with the person you are asking first. What you must have
> is a compelling story or product/service that would
> genuinely benefit the referral . . .

The fact that you had not cultivated a relationship with the person has become irrelevant because, more importantly, you had been in a position to help [your contact] benefit from the introduction. If it's of genuine benefit to the person being referred, I don't see the problem . . .

It's about the benefit of what's being referred rather than the relationship with the person asking for the referral . . . Who am I to deny my contacts of something good?"

Wow! What can I say? The "relationship" is irrelevant! All you have to have is a good story, product or service and I owe it to any stranger (who says he or she has a good product) to introduce him or her to a good contact of mine! ***Really?*** People ***really*** think this way!? According to this writer, it doesn't matter if I actually **know** or **trust** the person wanting the business. As long as the person has a good product (or so he says), I should refer that person because I would "deny" my contacts "something good!"

Networkers Against Premature Solicitation unite! We need to teach people that this is **NOT** a good way to network. Do YOU want to get hit up by people at networking events this way? Please tell me I'm not alone!

Networking is about relationship building–not "pouncing" on people because you think you have something good to sell them! Networking is not about hunting. It is about farming. It's about cultivating relationships. Don't engage in "premature solicitation." You'll be a better networker if you remember that.

Section 3:
Online Outlaws

"People do business first with those they like, know and trust. Social media is as simple as looking at it as a networking event without the need to drive there or the chance of getting cornered by the "creepy guy with scotch." It's about connection and conversation."

Scott Stratten,

UNMarketing:

Stop Marketing. Start Engaging

While the internet has transformed the world in so many ways, it has also proven to be a breeding ground for some of the *The World's Worst Networkers*. Social media sites are great and should be used with care and caution, as some of the best Reality Networkers® can turn into rogue, Online Outlaws, behaving in ways that repulse, reject and destroy relationships, reputations and businesses.

Chapter 20

The Twitter Twit

Bijay Shah

It was in Dubai that I met someone that I consider the "World's Worst Networker," who I will call "Doc." But I didn't encounter him at a business meeting or social event; it was on Twitter.

Twitter is a wonderful service and I use it for a number of reasons, one of which is to 'listen' to what others are saying about us and our business. The first time was when Doc posted a 'tweet' (i.e. a message, for those not familiar with Twitter-speak), saying that he had attended a BNI Chapter meeting, submitted an application to join and not heard from the committee for over 3 weeks.

I immediately got on the phone with the Membership Coordinator to find out what was happening and he confirmed to me that Doc indeed had visited 3 weeks ago. He was keen to join, filled in the application form and promised to submit his payment in a few days. Despite several follow-ups, he never did.

There are always 3 sides to a story so I investigated further. I checked the history of Doc's online activity and couldn't find much except for a few tweets posted a few months earlier. It seemed he was new in town and was finding it difficult to 'break in' the market. He was a medical practitioner (I'll not specify which medical profession to protect him) and instead of using his real name, he decided to use an alias which would create a perception that he was from a certain country.

His first tweet was *"can you talk about racism in Dubai? i am British but not accepted as such even though born there and English is my first language"*

A few weeks later, he happened to substitute for a colleague at another chapter. After the meeting, this is what he tweeted: *"substituted in BNI today for colleague did not get any referrals. In fact i have had no referrals at all!!!!"*

In BNI we know that certain professions take a longer time to build credibility and trust in order to be referred to. It seemed like Doc had no idea of this. He happened to have visited a BNI chapter as a substitute and expected to receive referrals that very day! Having spoken to some members for their feedback on him, they said he was too 'cold' and in his introduction, he talked about how well qualified he was. Because his focus was all about himself, I was reminded of that popular saying *"People don't care how much you know until they know how much you care."*

A few days later, I saw yet another tweet from Doc: *'I am really sterssed today, as you can see i am so stressed i can't spell!!!!'* Not only was this guy at the lowest point on my credibility curve, by now he had 'fallen off' the curve! Would you really trust a medical practitioner to treat you if he/she told you they were stressed!!

> *"Any fool can criticize, condemn and complain – and most do!" –*
> *Dale Carnegie*

Social media is an effective tool but as you can see from Doc's online behavior many people do not know how to use these tools effectively and are not aware of their power. I recently posted a question as a discussion in my Linked-In group on the use of Social Media tools when assessing someone. Over 80% of the respondents agreed that they would use tools such as Facebook, Twitter, LinkedIn and YouTube amongst others in the relationship building process to check and verify information on someone. With Online Networking and Social Media these days, you must be very cautious on how you conduct yourself. Would you do/say the things you do online in exactly the same way if you were off-line i.e. face-to-face?

The Internet Never Forgets

The New York Times Magazine reported:

> "[We live] in a world where the Internet records everything and forgets nothing — where every online photo, status update, Twitter post and blog entry by and about us can be stored forever. With Web sites like LOL Facebook Moments, which collects and shares embarrassing personal revelations from Facebook users, ill-advised photos and online chatter are coming back to

haunt people months or years after the fact.[11]"

Our parents taught us a valuable lesson when we were younger: that we should think carefully about our words before we actually say them. The same is true while we are networking online. We must approach it with the knowledge that everything we do or say online is recorded – forever, leaving a "virtual paper-trail". Twitter Twits like Doc seem to be ignorant or just do not care about the way they behave online.

The last tweet I saw from Doc read *'am looking to open my own clinic, let me know your thoughts for best location in dubai'.* His Twitter bio now reads: *'born, raised and educated in UK, NOW in Dubai'* and he has chosen not to show his real photo – this is what he has instead:

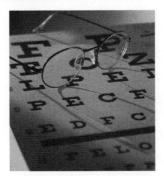

You can guess his medical profession I'm sure. While I wish him all the best in his practice, he should learn to practice being a better networker, both online and off, instead of acting out-of-line, online.

[11] Rosen, Jeffrey. "The Web Means the End of Forgetting." *New York Times Magazine.* New York Times, 21 July 2010. Web. 17 Aug. 2010. <http://www.nytimes.com/2010/07/25/magazine/25privacy-t2.html>.

Chapter 21

The Social Media Networking Stalker – What NOT To Do!

Sue Henry

I first saw his message on Facebook and ignored it. Then it showed up on Twitter. I ignored it. When it appeared on LinkedIn, I felt the Law of Attraction was at work and I clicked on the link. His social media marketing strategy was impressive. He used words that appealed to what I was looking for: "effective list building strategies resulting in a high conversion ratio".

A free teleseminar was being offered to share ideas, tips, and strategies on how to build a big list fast and convert a higher-than-average percentage of them into paying customers. I was intrigued and clicked on the link.

An opt-in screen requested my name, email (both are standard) and my phone number. I tried to register without adding the phone number but it was a required field. In order to be on the "free" call and receive some of this great information, I added my number and clicked to receive my email confirmation.

Problem #1: The top of the confirmation page was more of a sales page. As I scrolled down, there was a box requesting payment of $5. This was necessary to receive the teleseminar call-in instructions. The explanation was that the call was "free" and this $5 was to cover their admin costs. Because they made the information that was going to be shared sound so beneficial, I'm assuming that many people just clicked on it figuring, "what's $5"?

Problem #2: As I continued to read the fine print (felt like about a size 2 font), a written statement way at the bottom informed the person that they were giving permission to be billed $5 each month and you'd be included on the list of receiving information for the next "free" teleseminar. I was irritated that I had missed this information on their original marketing page, so I went back to see where the $5 fee was mentioned. It wasn't.

Problem #3: I signed out of the page and then wrote an email to the person about his unethical approach. Of course there was no response.

Problem #4: Within hours of logging off of the site, I receive an email telling me what a big mistake I'm making, how my business is going to close and that I'm going to become one of the "sad" statistics of a person who tries to use social media for business and fails miserably because of missing this incredible teleseminar. The message stated that if I sign up and give them the info for the $5 fee, they've got a free eBook they'll send me. I hit delete.

Problem #5: The following day I receive a phone call at the number I listed in the opt-in box from some "recording" telling me that I could be making millions if I follow the information given in the free teleseminar -- but space is limited and I need to call back and register immediately! I call back and leave a message to remove my name and number from their list.

Problem #6: A day later I receive another call. This time it's a real person and I'm extremely irritated. It's a sales person who works for a percentage of the $5. *(I have to wonder why someone would take a telemarketing job that paid $2.50 for each person who said yes... How many people could you realistically talk to in an hour? Just a thought...)* I ask to speak to the person in charge of this program. She gives me a number but it's the same number that I called and left a message with. I try again but only get voicemail.

Problem #7: That same day I receive a text telling me how I'm missing out, blah, blah, blah. Now I am furious! I text back and leave a message to never contact me again. I used very strong language.

Problem #8: A day later I received another email invite for the free teleseminar call and now the admin cost is $10. I've had it! No more Ms. Minnesota Nice!

Solution: I combined the email messages, including phone messages, times, dates, etc., and sent a complaint with all the accompanying information to LinkedIn and Facebook. That was more than a year ago and the marketing message of this company has not reappeared. I'm assuming they were shut down.

There are a lot of great marketers and networkers who successfully use social media to market their services and products. I've benefited greatly from being able to participate in their calls, receive eBooks, etc. Most social media marketers who make mistakes are new and are very coachable if someone will take the time to share why their method is going to backfire. They don't know what they don't know. Give them a chance and figure out how you can help them or refer them to someone who can. The best road is always the high road.

But once in a while someone comes along who is only concerned with increasing revenue and will use any method to do it, including stalking and intimidation. These are the people who need to be turned in so they can get "turned off".

Chapter 22

Are You More Than Just A Profile?

Jan Vermeiren

Many people are members of online business networks like LinkedIn, Ecademy, Xing, Twitter, and Facebook. LinkedIn, one of the preferred sites for business people, has over 97 Million members as of January 1, 2011[12]. Too often people have a tendency to join and then ask the questions, "Why on earth am I on this Web site?" and "How can I use it without spending too much time?"

Questions to Ask When Joining an Online Network:

Before joining an online network like LinkedIn, ask yourself "Can I treat my membership as I would with a membership in an off-line organization such as a business organization or networking group?" These are some valuable questions you can ask yourself before joining an online network:

- Why do I want to be a member of this particular network? Every social network is different in its focus. For example, Facebook is more social whereas LinkedIn is more business related. Both have members from around the world. Xing and Ecademy are similar to LinkedIn but have a more German, UK and European membership base.

---

[12] Source: http://www.linkedin.com/

You also need to decide if you can dedicate the time to devote to being an active member on these sites.

- What is my goal? You need to have clearly defined, specific goals when joining a social network. I like to think that a social network is like a car: you use it to reach specific destinations. If you were to just get in a car and drive, you could be driving around aimlessly, wasting gasoline, time and money. A social network is a tool to get you there but if you don't have a goal, the tool is worthless.

- Who do I want to meet? If you want to meet people for business purposes, consider LinkedIn, Xing or Ecademy. If you want to meet more people online who have similar interests as you, consider a site like Meetup.com. Meetup.com brings together people who have things in common at offline events referred to as "Meetups" in over 45,000 cities world-wide. To stay in touch and socialize with friends, family members and casual acquaintances, Facebook is the way to go.

- What do I want to learn or teach? Online networks bring people together from all over the world. Before you join, think about what subjects you would like to learn about or would like to teach others about.

The #1 Mistake Made When Joining An Online Network:

Very often, most people really do not know how to use LinkedIn and other social networking sites effectively. It is very common to hear people who have joined to say: "These networks don't work; I haven't got any customer via LinkedIn!" "Why doesn't anybody offer me a job? After all, my profile states that I'm looking for a new one." Others will just nod their head in agreement. When I ask them "how many people have you reached out to?" they usually remain silent. Some will reply with the excuse, "I don't have time to do that!" Yet, they expect others to take actions that they wouldn't do themselves.

One of the biggest misconceptions of some people who join online networks like LinkedIn is that once they join, they will automatically reach the contacts they want, get the job they are looking for or get referrals. While services like LinkedIn can provide amazing results in connecting with people from all over the world leading to opportunities to expand your network and your business, if you're just a profile, it's not going to happen that easily. Just like offline organizations, groups and networks, you need to be an active member.

Profiles vs. Active Membership.

Your online Profile can be very similar to your resume or C.V. You can fill out information and put it out for the world to see. But as a networking strategy, that is not very effective. Imagine as if you were one of tens of thousands of people who were competing for a new job. You can send a resume and hope that they will notice and call you for an interview. Rather than getting lost among all of the other profiles, you need to engage people by being an active member of the online community you participate in. People don't realize or they forget that when you join an online network, you need to use the same skill-sets as if you were networking in an offline organization.

Active online members do the following:

- **They interact with other members**. They listen to others and they answer questions about themselves. In this way they get to know each other and increase their KNOW-factor.

- **They help the other members** by giving them tips and connecting them with other members or with people from outside the organization. They do that without expecting anything in return. In this way they "add points" to their LIKE-factor.

- **They help the organization through volunteering and sharing their own knowledge and expertise**. In this way the TRUST-factor increases.

Just like if you pay a membership fee to go to a business networking group, but never show up, nothing much will happen. And even if you show up, but remain seated on a chair in a corner, not much will happen either. The same kind of dynamics applies to online networking. So here are some tips to remember:

1) **Create your profile.** Put enough information in your profile so that other people can find you and notice you. Don't just make it a resume or C.V. – expand on it and make yourself unique from others who share the same profession. If we compare LinkedIn to Facebook then you see that on LinkedIn 95% of the Profile is about business and Facebook 90% about personal things. LinkedIn is less active and interactive than Facebook, but for a business networking website that is OK.

2) **Reach out and connect people to each other**. When you think it would be beneficial for two people to know each other, be proactive and introduce them to each other. These can be people you already know and do business with but who may not know each other. On the other hand, they could be a source of interesting people, for you. On LinkedIn, once you connect with them, you can view each other's profiles and take a look at who their first line contacts are. Some of their contacts may be good potential clients for you. You can then talk to them at a meeting or other event and personally have a conversation such as, "I was just searching on LinkedIn and I saw you, and you knew Mr. X, my potential customer. How do you know him? What's your background?" And if you find out that they have a good relationship with the prospect, you could

ask "Would you be willing to make a referral or introduction?" Remember, you need to have conversations that are designed solely to sell or market your products or services.

3) **Join groups** and forums and be active in them. Answer questions and post your own questions. Don't just limit yourself to "business groups"; if you have a particular hobby or interest, find others who share the same or similar ones. Share experiences, help people and give them the opportunity to help you.

4) **Answer questions in your field of expertise** to develop your image as an expert in your field. One of the ways to stand out from others in your field is to obtain "expert status." If people perceive you as approachable and helpful, for instance, when you take the time to answer questions by others in your online network, you will be at the "top of their mind" when they or someone they know who may need your products or services.

5) **Give Testimonials and Recommendations to others:** One of the best features of LinkedIn is that you can recommend people in your network and provide testimonials. It helps people to have a higher trust and confidence level. Let's say I am looking for a potential customer. I connect with him through someone else, but they look at my LinkedIn profile and they see some

recommendations. If you have one recommendation, that might not be very helpful, but if you have 20 recommendations, then this person might already be more willing to do business with you. **A word of caution: I encourage and teach that people recommend each other, only if they have an experience or heard from their own network that this person is reliable.** It's not just, "Okay, let's do each other a favor;" it has to have a foundation.

By doing these actions you will create more visibility and credibility. Your "Know, Like and Trust Factor" will increase. What will happen next is probably *not* what you think that might happen: that some of the people you interact with become your customer or offer you a job. They probably won't. Instead, what they **WILL** do is talk about you to their network, resulting in many more customers or job offers over time.

Remember, online networking, just like "normal" networking, takes some time, but after the initial investment period it will bring much larger benefits in the long run.

Chapter 23

And Who Are You Today?
The Story Of The Two "Ernest" Networkers

Jerry Williamson

I live and work in what's referred to as the "Deep South" in the United States, where we are well known for our charm and warm hospitality to each other and to strangers. After owning my business for several years, I soon realized that I needed to market my company at local networking events and begin to become a part of the community if I wanted to give a face to my business.

I joined a local networking organization and then the local Chamber of Commerce. Both, were very good investments of my money and my time. I met some very affluent people in the community; I met some people who were very well connected, and some people who were willing to teach me the techniques to "proper" networking. But, I also met this one guy who seemed to be at every networking event I attended, who we will call Ernest.

Ernest was the "perfect" networker. He was at every networking event held in town, usually serving on the volunteer board for every event. He was great with greeting the guests, he seemed to know everyone, and the ladies just loved him. He was the endlessly gracious host at every event: he would bring people their cocktails, dance with all the ladies, and would go around, shaking hands in every corner of the room.

A new networking organization was started up in my hometown and Ernest was right there. From the very beginning, working hand in hand with the franchisee, helping them connects to the connectors.

He was a superstar!

EVERYONE loved Ernest!

Because I wanted to be accepted into the world of "master networkers," I was happy each time that Ernest would extend a handshake to me when I attended a networking event. When he started introducing me to some of the movers and shakers in town, I have to admit, I LOVED Ernest too – or at least, I wanted to. But something told me that things were too good to be true. There was something about Ernest that just didn't seem right. So I decided to sit back and observe Ernest for a while.

It wasn't long and Ernest requested to be my "friend" on one of the local social media sites. We would chat, and exchange funny stories, talk about business ideas. But even online, something just didn't seem right. For example, I began to question why Ernest didn't have his picture in his profile. Ernest would just reply that he didn't have a camera. (I thought to myself, who doesn't have a camera of some kind these days?). As time went on, I began to notice other things, like Ernest had a very vague profile; actually very little was filled out about himself.

And then one late Saturday evening, it happened.

Ernest went online and began to bash the entire group of people on the local social media site. The problem was that no one but me actually knew that it was Ernest! You see, without a picture, no one actually knew who Ernest was on the social media site. He even used a false name instead of his own.

Since I spent time with him, I observed that Ernest loved to drink scotch. Every now and then, Ernest would hit the scotch bottle *a little too much* and would soon transform into the drunken social media maven.

> *"Oh! what a tangled web we weave*
> *When first we practice to deceive!"*
> *- Sir Walter Scott, Marimon, Canto vi, Stanza 17*
> *Scottish author & novelist (1771 – 1832)*

As time went on, I began to notice that Ernest was relatively quiet on the social media sites except for when he's bashing people. (Remember: no one in the networking world knows who Ernest is on the social media site other than me because he doesn't have his picture in his profile and he requested that I become his friend under his pseudonym).

At this point, I am shocked and bewildered. I had to have talks with myself to try and make sense of how this great networker at networking events can become such a horrible, mean person when he is anonymously hitting the scotch bottle; but being "new" to the networking scene and understanding the incredible power of word-of-mouth, I kept it myself, not wanting to be the one to spread rumors.

As time went on, I began to notice people here and there are starting to talk about Ernest. At first, the stories described how Ernest would be rude when he visited someone's store; but then the stories became more serious, how he began to bounce checks on people or avoid their calls. People were getting angry, but again, not being one to want to cause a raucous, I kept quiet and continued to observe.

Then the day came that I couldn't hold back anymore. Ernest decides to bash one of my friends on the social media site. Now my gloves came off and I had to confront him.

When I had a chance, I privately told Ernest how he should not bash people online and how I was offended that he was publicly bashing one of my friends. Ernest replied with very rude finger gesture. I'm shocked not knowing what to say or how to react. (Now, mind you I'm thinking how I should react, but being the professional that I am, I refrained).

Immediately after our meeting, Ernest had a new target to his social media hit list: **ME**! As people started to see him bash me, his secret online identity was becoming more and more known. As the web continued to be unwoven, people began to notice how dysfunctional this person actually was.

Ernest's hit-list began to grow. In no time, the very networking franchise that he helped build membership during its infancy was soon the target of his destruction. He began to bash and attack the franchise owner online, and even went so far as to to call and harass her at home by leaving cryptic, "anonymous" messages and by sending her threatening emails. Ernest was working his back-door, black magic to slowly destroy the very

organization he helped to build, while at the same time, keeping a
very charming, public profile with the local business community.

As time goes on, word-of-mouth begins to circulate
throughout the networking community that Ernest is a trouble
maker. During the long, hot summer his social media hit-list
grows and grows, and there doesn't seem to be an end in sight.

Until early one balmy southern Saturday morning, Ernest
decides to hit the scotch bottle. While blitzed and missing several
thousand brain cells, he decided to take on an attorney on the
local social media site. What Ernest didn't realize was that he had
made so many enemies that his "secret online" identity, was no
longer a secret.

The attorney didn't take the online bashing "lying down."
Instead, he began a private investigation of Ernest and his
background. In no time, the story of the "secret networker"
finally comes to light: that Ernest was not only a mean-hearted
person, but actually had been ran out of town for the last two
places he lived in, leaving behind a multitude of debt along with
dozens of "secret identities."[13] You can imagine how everyone in
the "circle" was talking about Ernest, all while he had no idea that
his online "secret identity" has been revealed.

What seemed to be consuming a major part of my life and
that of others in the business community, now appears to have
been nature's way of slowly untangling the web that Ernest had so

---

[13]   Please understand that I have condensed about 4 months of
networking neighborhood drama into a few pages.

carefully and diligently woven. His world seems to be slowly falling apart.

Within the 4 month time span that the social networking faux pas occurred, Ernest was once again slowly demystified and bounced from job to job, leaving behind his now obvious venomous trail of survivors. It wasn't long before Ernest called one of his targets for some scotch-driven harassing and the phone call was interrupted by her husband!

Coming to her rescue, the husband informs Ernest that he had checked out his background and knew exactly where he lived and would love to make a visit some sunny Sunday afternoon for "some tea." (In other words, ole Ernest was about to get some good old fashioned, butt kickin'). Soon, another networking organization gets wind of the turmoil Ernest is creating within the community and they, along with the Chamber of Commerce, choose to remove him from their organizations, at the same time. Soon thereafter, Ernest is no longer the playboy of networking, but the "world's worst networker." As Ernest's world rapidly falls apart, the negative word-of-mouth caused him to lose his job.

Important Lessons I Learned from Being with Ernest:

Your network is a statement about who you are and what you stand for. The people in your network reflect your belief system. Always be willing to take the time to build a relationship with your contacts *before* you trust them with your best clients, family members, and friends, both online and offline. You'll be glad you did.

Ernest is currently working at the local convenience store as the night shift clerk. I like to stop in and visit with him every now and then, just to remind myself of how I should always follow my gut and sit back and observe before I add people to my network.

(And, one last word of advice: stay away from the scotch!)

Section 4:
From A Mess To A Success:
Strategies and Stories To Make You A
Better Networker

"Success is a science; if you have the conditions, you get the results."

— Oscar Wilde

Not everyone was born a natural networker. Even some of the best networkers in the world were once among the world's worst. The advice, strategies and secrets shared in the following stories and experiences will inspire and help transform even *The World's Worst Networker* into one of the *world's best!*

Chapter 24

Networking Faux Pas

Ivan Misner, Ph.D.

After two decades of running the world's largest networking organization, I have certainly seen a lot of networking faux pas. A networking faux pas is a slip or blunder in networking etiquette or conduct. I have put together a few of the most glaring ones that I've seen over the years so that you might avoid them in your networking efforts.

Faux Pas #1: Not responding quickly to referral partners.

This one really troubles me. I cannot imagine getting a call from a networking partner and not responding immediately, but unfortunately, it seems to happen with some regularity. Not long ago, someone I know had a referral for a gentleman in his networking group. He called the associate and left a message at his office as soon as he knew the referral was viable. A day went by without a return call, so he called again saying it was important to connect.

He was finally able to speak to his networking associate at their next meeting. He asked him why he did not return his call and the associate said: "If I knew you had a referral for me, I would've called you back immediately." He did give the referral at the meeting and to no one's surprise the referral ended up working with another vendor because no one got back to him in a timely manner.

Treating each of your networking partners as one of your "best clients" is critical. You should always return phone calls from these people immediately, as it speaks to your credibility and reliability as a professional.

There have been countless examples of people receiving referrals at networking groups who go back to their places of business and finally get around to contacting the referral in a few days. The old phrase, "if you snooze, you lose" is apropos here. Time is of the essence and if the referral knows that you had her name and number on Monday and you took your sweet time calling that sends a message you don't want to be sending!

Faux Pas #2: Confusing networking with direct selling.

One of our BNI Directors struck up a conversation with a woman business owner at a networking function; when the business owner asked our Director what she did, she told her that she helps business owners build their business through networking and referrals. The business owner smiled and said, "I'm really good at networking! I've been doing it for a long, long time."

Curious, our Director asked her, "So what's your secret?" She stood up straight and said, "Well, a friend and I enter a room together. We imagine drawing a line down the middle. She takes the left side, I take the right side. We agree to meet back together at a certain time to see who collected the most cards! The loser buys the other one lunch."

The Director curiously inquired, "so what do you do with all those cards?" Again, proudly, the business owner expressed, "I enter them into my distribution list and begin to send them information about my services! Since I have all their information, they're all good prospects, right?"

This is a classic example of an entrepreneur not understanding that networking is not about simply gathering contact information and following up on it at a later date. That is nothing more than glorified cold calling! Brrrrr, it gives me the chills! I used to teach cold calling techniques to business people. I did it enough to know that I didn't want to ever do it again. I have devoted my entire professional life to teaching the business community that there is a better way to build long-term business.

Faux Pas #3: Abusing the relationship.

There are many ways that I've seen networking partners abuse the relationship, but the following story is absolutely one of the most glaring examples of this situation.

A woman I know was invited to attend a 50th birthday party of an associate who used to belong to a networking group in which she also participated. They once had a long-term working relationship, and so out of respect, she decided to attend. When she got to the door, she looked through the window and noticed that people were arranged in a semi-circle listening to a presenter in front of an easel board. When she stepped in, it was very obvious that the "party goers" were being recruited for a business opportunity. As resentful as the woman felt, she and other mutual friends found it difficult to remove themselves from the "birthday party" despite the fact that the only refreshments being served was the company's diet shake!

<u>Never</u>, <u>ever</u> mislead your networking partners (for that matter – never mislead anyone). Trust is *everything* when you are talking about relationship networking. Inviting these people to a "birthday party" which turns out to be a business opportunity is not being honest with the very people with whom you want to build a trusting relationship.

All of these faux pas directly relate to good people skills. The prevailing theme of all three is to treat your referral partners (or potential referral partners) with professionalism and care. Make sure to respond to them quickly, don't treat a networking opportunity like a cold-call, and don't abuse a networking relationship. Instead, treat your referral partner like you would a #1 client. Use networking opportunities to meet people and begin the process of developing a genuine relationship.

Lastly, always network in a way that builds credibility and trust – be candid in telling your referral partners what you need and what you're asking of them. Do these things and you'll help to avoid some serious mistakes in relationship networking.

Chapter 25

Control Your Referral Flow

Tim Houston

One of the biggest challenges for networkers who have a small operation regardless of their profession, is that they can find themselves overwhelmed with receiving too many referrals from their networking efforts. In their haste, too many make the fatal mistakes of stopping their networking and they tell everyone to stop giving them referrals. Not only did they voluntarily join the ranks of *The World's Worst Networker*, but they ultimately end up at a time in the future with little or no business. People assume that they no longer want referrals. In the worst case, they even cut themselves off from their referral sources.

A few years ago, I went to a local networking group. They were excited to have a new plumber in their group, who I will call Artie. In talking to Artie, I found out that his business was a two man operation; he and his brother managed the business, did the technical work on each job and also did the marketing for the business. He was happy to be a part of the group which also had a general contractor, an electrician and a painter who shared a similar client base as his own. As the meeting progressed, I watched Artie get at least 6 referrals that day. He left the meeting very happy.

Two months later, I visited the group and towards the end of the meeting, Artie stood up and announced that this would be his final meeting. People were surprised and shocked to hear it. He explained that he was getting *too many referrals* – more than he and his brother could handle! It did not leave a good impression with most people as they interpreted this to mean that all he wanted to do was score a "quick hit" and move on.

Later that day, I called Artie and asked if I could speak to him about his decision. Since Artie was a plumber, I used the analogy that, just like in plumbing, you need to learn how to control the flow. I explained that in networking, just like in plumbing, there are certain "valves" or "taps" that are used with "knobs" which can adjust how fast or slow the referrals will flow.

Control #1: Tell your network *when* to give you referrals.

One October morning a decorative artist and designer told the members at his weekly networking meeting that a good referral would be "a person who is looking for a decorative mural in their home or business any time after February 1st." He explained that he had too many jobs to handle at the moment but was booking jobs that would start in February. The designer had the presence of mind to let his network know to keep the referrals coming – just not the kind that needed his services right now. In effect, he was keeping his pipeline full so that he didn't experience a referral shortage once the jobs he was currently working on were completed.

Control #2: Refer your "overflow" work to someone you trust in your profession.

If you find yourself with too many referrals, before turning away the business, talk to both the source and the person being referred and let them know that, although you can't handle the work now, you know someone else in your profession who could. Make sure that you introduce the prospect to your collaborator and ask to stay involved with the progress. The impression you will make on both the source of the referral and the prospect will help you in the long-run. Also, your collaborator will likely remember you and refer work to you when they are experiencing overflow.

Control #3: Prevent Back-flow.

Back-flow occurs when there's a drop of pressure and contaminated water begins to flow from the ground or a storage system into the clean water system of the building or water supply. In plumbing, there are devices known as "check valves" which prevent this from happening. Artie thought that if he stopped the flow of referrals at the source, (i.e. if he quit), it would provide him with the breathing room he needed to catch up. Once that happened, he believed he could return to networking. I replied that he was actually creating back-flow.

In networking, negative word-of-mouth results in back-flow. Too often this will occur when someone takes on a job that they cannot handle, causing problems, delays, and headaches resulting in ill-will for all involved. It also occurs when people perceive that the person only cares about themself.

In Artie's case, he received a lot of referrals and the people in his networking group saw his quitting as giving up on them. They became "contaminated" with the notion that all Artie wanted was to take from the table and not give anything in return. I suggested that one way he could install a "check valve" to prevent the back-flow was to give referrals to others and to introduce them to potential referral partners and sources for their respective businesses.

In the end, Artie decided to stick it out and to put these suggestions into practice. A year later, he is still active in his networking group; he has been giving referrals regularly and has introduced people to other potential sources and referral partners. He told me that learning to control his referral flow has helped him to expand his business: he now has two new plumbers working for him and an administrative assistant. Because of a referral for a simple job (a hot water heater installation), Artie recently landed an account to be the plumber for a high-rise apartment building! He realized that he probably would not have received this referral had he given up and walked away from his networking group and referral sources.

Chapter 26

You DO NOT Have To Take Every Interview Or Networking Meeting
Caroline Ceniza-Levine

As a career coach, I believe that networking is a very important activity in helping people to find jobs or to enhance their careers, as well as for those who want to take the step in venturing out in starting a new business. As a business owner, I value networking as a vehicle to promote my business to recruiters, human resource administrators and even college career programs, in addition to creating and enhancing relationships with others who could refer potential clients. But one of the worst mistakes made by job seekers and business networkers is to try to do it all.

As a general rule, I do encourage people to accept interview and meeting invitations. Even if you are not interested in the job now, you may become interested as you learn more. You meet new people which could lead to other opportunities. You learn about what other companies are doing. Even when you're happily employed, it's useful to know your market and get a sense for your value.

That said, we all have limited time and energy. We physically can't network 24/7, either in person, or online, nor should we. There may be other things that are more important, even for jobseekers and businesspeople. Here are 3 examples of when you might want to decline a meeting:

1. The invitations you are getting are off-target. In the beginning of a job search or when you are new to networking, it is hard to know if an invitation fits your objectives or not. It is worth it to say yes to mostly anything because you need to get out there, practice interacting, and get a firsthand feel of your market. But after a few weeks, you should review who you've been meeting: are they in and around the industry/ functional areas that I am targeting? Are they in a position to hire me or refer me? At the very least, are these people that I want to develop relationships with? It shouldn't be about who can help you (that's too narrow a view for networking) BUT you do want to have genuine interest in people. If you are getting invitations that are far afield from your interests and you are dreading these meetings, it's worth it to decline the meetings and spend the time you save figuring out why you are not attracting the right people.

2. You need to focus on follow up, rather than meeting more people. Most people don't make enough time for meeting new people, but there are some out there who network so much it is like busy work for them. They flit out and about to every mixer and meeting and justify this haphazard activity as important networking. Networking is not just about meeting more and more people. It is also about deepening relationships with people you have met before. If you have made a lot of contacts already, your time may be better spent getting back to those contacts, rather than adding more. In an ideal schedule, you reserve time for both, so make sure you indeed do both expanding and maintaining your network.

3. There are more time-sensitive things to do

now. Perhaps your business is overwhelmed with work and cannot keep up with client orders or demands; maybe there are health or child-care issues that take precedent over everything else. Maybe you were just hired by your company and you haven't had a chance to settle into your new role and you are still learning the basics of your profession. It doesn't matter if you are a recent graduate, a small business owner or professional at a Fortune 500 big company: sometimes you try to do too many things and lose focus on priorities

I once presented a time management workshop at a company that was undergoing a major restructuring. People were juggling multiple roles, including brand new areas. The first point I made (and you could hear the sigh of relief) was that everything else should be tabled for the next 90 days as this overhaul went through – I pointed out family balance may go out of whack, social outings may have to be curtailed, even sleep may take a hit. This was a crunch time for this group. They needed to push through, with almost tunnel-vision, and then they could reassess. Obviously, if the restructuring is open-ended, this is not a long-term solution. But there will be times when there is a time-sensitive crunch of activity that needs to come first, and even important things like networking need to be set aside. As Dr. Stephen Covey wrote in *The 7 Habits of Highly Effective People:* "The key is not to prioritize what is on your schedule, but to schedule your priorities."

You're Not Excused From Networking!

People should not use excuses to get off the hook in this sometimes uncomfortable endeavor. The fact remains that most people don't do enough productive networking. The best networkers know that not all networking is *good networking;* the worst networkers tend to equate action with progress. They go from event to event, spinning their wheels or using "networking" as busy work to avoid other more important activities. They may be fearful that by not attending an interview or a networking event will result in some kind of a loss. The result is that they overload themselves unnecessarily and burn out.

Remember, networking is necessary; any one meeting is not. Learn to make proactive choices, not reactive, to assess where you are in your business and relationships with others.

Chapter 27

Having The Hard Conversation

Kevin Snow

A successful networker knows that networking helps to build a community of relationships. Over time, as people bond with one another, it is not uncommon to hear members of business and networking groups or professional organizations describe themselves as being "friends" or tell others how the group has become "like a family." Just like a successful marriage or family life, open and honest communication between the members of the group is the key to an enduring, fulfilling, robust, relationship. But when there is a lack of communication or if a member feels estranged or otherwise alienated by others in the group, it sets the stage for a bitter confrontation and quite possibly, a divorce.

At one of the regular meetings of a business organization I belong to, one of the members, (we will call him Mike), came to me with issues he was having with another member, Kathy. After I listened to his comments, I asked him a simple question, "Have you talked to Kathy about this?" He said no. From conversations I had with the leaders of the group, I learned that Mike had been having similar conversations with multiple people in the group trying to get them to talk to Kathy for him. Mike missed a great opportunity to build a stronger relationship with someone he networked with regularly.

> *"It is tact that is golden, not silence"*
> *– Samuel Butler, British Poet (1835-1902)*

Many of us grew up hearing from our parents and teachers, "If you don't have anything nice to say, don't say anything at all." But that philosophy on communication and relationships only masks the issues that people may have with each other. It is always easier to always talk about the positive things going on in our work and relationships than to have a frank conversation about issues that are bothering us. Confrontation isn't fun, but it is these conversations that tend to lead to a stronger relationship and better understanding between the two people involved.

Mike's tactic of trying to illicit supporters instead of going directly to Kathy to talk out the issues didn't have the effect that he was hoping for. Instead of getting help to fix the issue, Mike actually hurt the trust and credibility he had developed with his network. He showed them that if something went wrong, he wouldn't talk to them to fix it; he would instead tell all the people around them. Would you want to refer clients or family to someone where you knew that they may end up telling your other referral partners negative things about you without giving you a chance to rectify the situation?

From a Group that "Clicked" to a Group of Cliques:

By talking to everyone other than Kathy, Mike also successfully shifted the personality of the group from that of a successful business networking group to the personality of a high school clique or a coffee clutch. The gossip that was running rampant in the group also had a terrible impact on Kathy. The situation deteriorated to the point that she felt she needed to leave the group as her reputation and credibility had been damaged so much that she wouldn't be able to get the quality referrals she was used to getting. It was also having an impact on others, forcing them to take sides and ruining strong relationships that where in place for many years, among many of the members.

Having the Hard Conversation:

When these situations arise, it is important to approach these conversations with the right attitude no matter what side of the conversation you are participating on. The wrong attitude and approach can lead to hurt feelings and an outcome similar to what Mike and Kathy experience. Here are four things to keep in mind when you are faced with having a "hard conversation".

1. Talk in Private.

Praise in public, coach in private. If you are members of an organization together, please refrain from approaching them at your meeting and launching into a list of things you want them to do different. Doing that will actually have a negative impact on how the rest of the group sees you along with diminishing the impact on the person you are talking to as they will feel embarrassed and try to end the conversation as quickly as possible. Instead, take the person you need to talk to out for a cup of coffee or lunch. Have the conversation on neutral territory so that neither party appears to have "home field advantage".

2. **Always say "Thank You!"**

When you start the private conversation with the person, always start by telling them that you appreciate their efforts to help you. More often than not, the individual really is just trying to help you and thinks that they actually are. You need to let them know that you appreciate them thinking of you *before* you start trying to adjust their behavior. If you don't thank them, you risk them not wanting to help you in the future.

3. **Ask.**

Always ask if they are open to some suggestions or coaching. Having them say yes to this question opens the door for you to help them help you more effectively without having as much push-back or defensiveness.

4. **Be Open to Suggestions.**

This is really for the person receiving the suggestion but can apply to the person giving them as well. Getting defensive only puts up walls between the individuals talking and prevents people from actually hearing what the other person is saying. Remember that the person giving the suggestions is talking to you because they value the relationship they have with you and want to make it better and they have identified something that in their mind is hindering that. Conversely, the person receiving the suggestions may have suggestions of their own that they make and we need to be open to them as well.

Networking requires interactions and conversations of all kinds. Having the hard conversation with someone can be stressful to think about but having it and approaching it in a positive way with the right attitude can make the results more beneficial to each person involved rather than just living with the status quo. Don't throw away an opportunity to make a good relationship a great relationship!

Chapter 28

The Once Timid Networker

Tara Schmakel

I've had the entrepreneurial spirit since I was 6, when I started my first business. Over the years, my methods and businesses may have changed but my enthusiasm has always remained child-like. I always knew that networking was very important to my business' growth and development, however, one thing always hindered my networking efforts. I was a person who felt easily intimidated and shy, especially when I networked. In short, I was a very Timid Networker. My efforts could have been more productive but I was getting in my own way.

I honestly thought of myself as being one of the worst networkers in the world, but if my business was to grow and expand, I knew that I had to do something. I resolved to do this and transformed myself into *The Once Timid Networker*. The journey would be a challenge but I was as driven as I was timid and I knew it would be worth it! Little by little, it was going to happen, over time, with a little help from my friends. I'd like to share two of the most important and memorable experiences in my networking efforts that helped make my transformation possible and the lessons I learned from each.

Experience #1: The Intimidated, Timid Networker:

Six years ago, I joined BNI, in the greater-Minneapolis,

Minnesota area, representing my custom interior design business, *The Workroom at Tara's.* I was very timid at my chapter meetings, but I knew that this was the place I needed to be to grow my business. As much as I loved BNI's concept and *Giver's Gain*® philosophy, I initially disliked our weekly meetings because it was not in my nature to talk to people I didn't know. Each week, on my 30 minute drive to the meetings, I would usually practice my 60 second presentation I had prepared; but I would also think thoughts that were so destructive: who will I talk to? What if nobody talks to me? By the time I arrived at the meeting, I was sick to my stomach with anxiety.

In the beginning of my BNI experience, I grew to absolutely loath the "Open Networking" part of the meeting where members and guests interact with each other during the first 15 minutes. For a timid person like me, it seemed like an eternity. There were a few times I summoned the courage to walk over to another circle of people, but usually ended up feeling more ridiculous than I did already. Although they acknowledged my presence, they didn't include me in the conversation. So my "networking strategy" became very simple: I would arrive and put my things down at the seat I had selected then scan the room for three things: 1) the nearest escape, 2) the coffee and treats, and 3) a possible friendly face.

When the Student is Ready, the Teacher Will Appear:

One day Wayne, another member of the chapter, caught

my eye and waved across the room to me. He was an older gentleman with a very kind eyes and a warm smile. He was so friendly and I realized I could always go to his side and he would welcome me into the conversation. With time, I became more relaxed and at ease at being a member of this chapter, which led me to be less intimidated by others.

About a year later, a friend of mine who was a BNI Director, had asked me to fill in for him at a group that was in the process of becoming a BNI chapter. I silently thought he must have been desperate for help and I must have been on cold medication that day since I said I would help him! I have no idea why he asked *me* or why I said yes. He handed me a sheet of paper that said "Mentoring checklist" which I reviewed. I put on my best "pretend-a-ambassador" face and went to teach this group about being a mentor and what it could mean to a new member.

As I prepared for this and researched the material for my presentation, it touched my heart and stirred my soul. I realized that although I was part of a larger chapter even among a small group of about 20 people, there were some who felt scared or timid at their initial BNI meetings. This caused me to reflect on the way that Wayne had treated me, his warmth and how he always seemed happy to see me. Wayne was always approachable and made me feel as though I belonged there at that meeting. When I had a question, I knew I could ask him. When there were trainings coming up, he asked if I would like to join the group that was going. I thought, what if every member – be it in a newly forming chapter or in an existing chapter -- had their own mentor like my friend Wayne?

Shortly after that experience, I accepted the role of ambassador with the sole purpose of teaching chapters the value of being a mentor. In short period of time, we have researched and modified the program and have developed a system that is incredible and that our region is very proud of, especially for those timid people who were like me.

Experience #2: The Turtle

One day, I saved a pretty little turtle who was trying to cross the very busy road I live on. I saw it crossing and felt the need to go help. There were cars racing by and I cringed each time one would pass, for fear it would run over that scared little turtle. I waited for the right moment, ran into the street and grabbed it by its shell. I got to the other side of the road and placed it by some wetlands that are nearby. I felt so good that when I got back into my house, I had to post it on Facebook!

For days, I thought of my experience and then out of nowhere I figured out why: **I could relate to that little turtle!** It had a goal, to get to the other side of the road. It was taking the steps to accomplish that goal but was having a hard time reaching it. It would take a few slow steps but then a car would race over it and it would start to turn around to come back. It was as if fear was making it turn back even though the goal was in sight.

As *The Once Timid Networker*, I used to attend networking events and behave just like that turtle. I had the goal, I knew what to do, but as soon as I was surrounded by other networkers racing around, exchanging business cards, making appointments in their calendars, and talking to others I would get nervous and overwhelmed and fear would take over. At times, I even tried to head back to the door just so I could get away. Have you ever felt that way? Have you ever observed someone feeling that way?

Becoming The Shadow:

Like that turtle, I needed assistance to reach my goal. I began to realize that if I could be open and honest with a trusted friend or two, they could be my rescuers and help me when I needed it. I enlisted the help of two friends of mine, Chad and Steve. At first I was their shadow. I stayed close, met the people they met and moved on when they moved on. I observed every detail, the questions they asked, what they did with the business cards they collected, even their body language. I wanted to be as comfortable as they were and move through the room effortlessly, like they did.

It became easier and gradually I would move away to talk to someone but then come back to my rescuers side. I made it my goal to venture out and try to meet one new person. The next time I wanted to meet two new people. I did this over a period of time, at different networking events, and then one day I realized something changed.

Breaking Away

I went to a networking event and discovered my rescuers, Chad and Steve, had arrived before me. As usual, I was mentally prepared to play the role of their shadow, having become very comfortable in that tidy little box of mine. As I walked into the venue, I noticed they were at opposite corners, on the other side across a very crowded room. Normally, I'd rush over to one of them, but this time, I did something different.

We waved and nodded to each other when our eyes met. I looked around the room and got my bearings. However this time, I refrained from rushing to their side. Instead I looked for the new person in the room – the timid one – the one who was overwhelmed and paralyzed in the middle of the room, the person that I usually was at these events. I spotted one and made my way to them.

In talking to the person, I learned, like me, they too had their goal. That was why they were there. But just like I used to, they were eyeing the door with that all too familiar gaze. I wanted to help them feel at ease the way my rescuers had helped me, so I offered to stay with them and introduce them to some of the people that I knew. I was doing exactly the same thing that Chad and Steve did for me for my new friend, who before they left, expressed their sincere thanks to me.

When I went home that night, I realized I never did share

more than a sentence or two with my friends Chad and Steve. I felt a little sad and missed them because being by their side had become such a habit. And yet I was proud because I realized I had grown and had broken free from being their shadow.

Invaluable Lessons Learned:

The lessons I learned from my experiences with Wayne, Chad and Steve were invaluable to my networking experience. Whether it's at a formal networking group like a BNI chapter, a business card exchange or any other social function, find that lost soul. The one who can't or won't make eye contact and they're wringing their hands. The one standing (or sitting) at their seat. They are looking for a reason to get the heck out of there! Give them a reason to stay. Help them to feel comfortable and at ease. You may be giving them something that they have never experienced before. You might be pivotal in their success.

Now it is my time to pay-it-forward. Every time I go to a networking event, I make it a point to go look for more "turtles" and I do my best to be a mentor to people who are new to networking. I might be the one who makes a difference for that person like Wayne, Chad and Steve did for me. Like the turtle, Chad and Steve had helped me cross the busy networking road and Wayne showed me the value of being a mentor and in being welcoming and friendly to people. Each of them had helped me reach my goals and for that I am so grateful. Without their help, I may have never become, *The Once Timid Networker*.

Chapter 29

Bird Of Prey

Elaine Betts

Circling, spiraling, gliding through air,

Beady eyes glancing for their next prey to snare.

Moving with purpose, but not always right,

Their victim or target is now in their sight.

With ease they dive forward, a firm grasp at hand,

Their presence is awkward and the view they command.

Ruffles n shuffles to swoop into place

Jump into a sentence that's right in your face

Shortsighted in nature a hunter of course,

Killer instinct reaction with little remorse.

Capture their target, engulf them with pain,

Poor victim has no chance, life's blood they will drain.

The sad part about it, they don't even know

They're hurting their business and preventing it grow

Open your eyes and look deep and true

Take heed of your actions, make sure it's not you.

Our fate is determined by all that we're being

Notice your actions be sure you are seeing

Bring forth the farmer who knows to sow seed,

They look to the future with no count of greed.

Bird of prey actions kick right out the door

Build long lasting connections so business can soar

Farmers in business who sow seed today,

Have a successful future, and a chance to make hay.

What is it about some business owners and the way they network that just leave us absolutely gobsmacked and wishing that we had never ventured outdoors!!!

I have a bearded dragon, well it's not mine actually, it's my son's pet, but as he is at university, I have inherited it. Her name is Delilah and Delilah needs a certain amount of sunlight every week otherwise, just like humans she gets a vitamin deficiency which leads to poor health. She loves the sunshine, you can see it's her life blood, stretching her neck and head up and basking contentedly in the sunshine. That is of course until she sees a bird flying overhead, and then she flattens her body so quickly, her color changes to blend in more with her surroundings and she tilts her head slightly so that one of her eyes can see full on the bird above her. She remains so still and flat, her beady eye traverses the sky until the bird has flown by. Wriggling flatter and flatter she concentrates and thinks of nothing else, she's in survival mode, protecting her life until the danger has passed.

You may be asking yourself "What does this have to do with business?" Well, how often do we feel like Delilah when going to a networking event or professional gathering? There are some business professionals who have no clue about business etiquette and as good as they might be in their respective field or profession, they do not realize just how much business is being missed out on because of their actions. Other business owners are melting into the background and trying desperately to camouflage themselves and hide from the *Bird Of Prey*.

A business owner's life blood could be a networking event, just like the sunshine is to Delilah. It may be in the form of a chamber mixer, a professional association meeting or a conference where people gather to make connections, learn professional information and build their credibility. Either way, a business professional has to 'step outside into the sunshine' to remain healthy.

All too often though just like Delilah when we step outside into the sunshine our heart starts to sink and our focus is not on the original purpose of the event or in Delilah's case enjoying the sunshine, because there they are, the vultures, those *annoying Birds Of Prey*, circling around the room. It is not possible to concentrate on anything else other than survival and not being captured by this associate's grasp. We end up spending more time focusing on trying to avoid them and blending in with the crowd. Our focus ends up on not who we want to meet, but more, how we can stave off or remain out of sight of the vultures. What is important though is that we are not put off in venturing out into the sunshine as this serves no positive outcome for the wellbeing of our business.

Am I a Bird Of Prey?   How can I be a better networker?

There are occasions in our lives when we all have been a *Bird Of Prey* just because we were caught up in a moment of enthusiasm or shear passion of what we were looking to achieve. We just know that what we have to offer or say is the "best thing since sliced bread." We want to share the information, product or service and we genuinely believe that whoever we are speaking to will absolutely need or want this too. It might not even be a product or service, it could be a belief or opinion that we have or hold, so it is important to be mindful that we can also be a *Bird Of Prey* outside of our professional life too and be a *Bird Of Prey* in our social circles. If we do this just now and again, our friends and colleagues will forgive us. They will probably smile and say to one another there they go again, all gung ho and fired up. But if this is a consistent action or behavior that is taken, then it becomes damaging to our character, relationships and professionalism.

When we first start out in business and networking, we are naïve; of course we make mistakes, of course we are enthusiastic and as we become better networkers we look back maybe and cringe at our inexperience and lack of tact. That's ok we all started somewhere and learning by experience and watching how successful people work is key.

Sometimes it is easier to see the actions that we are **not** doing rather than what we are doing.

1. **Listening**- if we are not listening to other people, then chances are we are not present to what is going on around us. This can be very frustrating for those who are around us at that time. Not being present also means missed opportunities. Are we truly listening to our colleagues? Go on, be brave ask a few of your closest connections that you have a good relationship with. *Do you think I am always listening to other people?*

2. **Giving the other person a chance to speak**- If we are speaking too much, it becomes a very one sided conversation and people will soon tire of you. Again this also means a lack of understanding for what is going on around you and being present. I know I can talk, but sometimes there are people out there where you just can't get a word in edgeways. They don't even seem to stop to breath and come up for air. You find yourself fascinated in how on earth do they keep talking for so long without breathing, you know the people I mean, you've met them too! I find I want to get the stop watch out and see when they come up for air, by this time though I've no clue what they are talking about anyway I'm just in awe of their breathing capabilities!!!

3. **<u>Not being aware</u>** – being enthusiastic about something is
one thing, but when we are oblivious to the people around
us we can become insensitive to the situation and that can
be the end of a potential relationship if we are not careful.
Someone may have just had some terrible news and need a
friendly gesture of support or empathy with a situation,
this is the time to listen and help if appropriate and curb
your own enthusiasm.

You do not have to be a novice networker to be a bird of
prey, we can transform into one very easily at any stage of our
careers. When we get so caught up, enthusiastic or engrossed in
what we are trying to accomplish we forget to listen to other
people around us. We do not mean to, it's just that we are so
enthusiastic about what we are currently doing we blurt out in
rapid fire with no consideration for what the other people around
us are experiencing. Be present and become aware of the actions
being taken. Step back from this situation, stop and ask the other
people around you what has been a highlight of their week.

When I asked this question of someone at an event who
had been sat there very quietly, not really saying very much at all,
it was like a light switch turning on the light, their whole face lit
up. They had just become a proud grandparent and they just
gushed with conversation, they began to speak enthusiastically
and share in the conversation, it made their evening, and I had a

very different relationship with this person, a bond of friendship had formed.

4 **Not building a relationship** – do we not have any patience and jump right in and ask for referrals and demand business straight away? We've seen this too, the croupier of business card distribution, who hands out their cards as if they were dealing cards for black jack saying 'here's my card I do ….. and everyone needs my services so let's get together I'm happy to look at your documents and I'll save you some money' …errrrr " what's your name, and how many minutes since I met you"!!!! We can hurt our reputation so very badly by bull dozing, we have no idea what the other person wants or if we are a good fit for them. Ask some qualifying questions before you leap in. If their brother or sister or dearest school friend that they have known for decades does what you do, forget it, see how you can help them in others ways before pushing your trade down their throat, you never know, they may refer other people to you over time. Think long term.

Strategy!

What do you do if you end up caught in the grips of a continual *Bird Of Prey*? You've been caught, and are in their clutches, now what? For the driver personality it's probably not too difficult for you to extract yourself from the conversation, it might be a nice gesture though not to burn bridges or leave them in the dust as road kill!! For the rest of the population though this maybe a tricky and unpleasant circumstance and may not feel comfortable just cutting them off. Here are some suggestions and approaches that might work for you.

3 Ways to Tactfully Help The *Bird of Prey* Work On Their Professionalism.

1.Encourage them to take a fantastic class

If you have recently taken a class, or know someone who has, encourage them to take the class that you have recently taken or heard of that increases sales, works on building better connections and relationships or customer service. Please add in here whatever relevant professional subject matter that is relevant as some *birds of prey* are not looking to increase their sales, they may just have their own opinions, but a good healthy workshop on how to work with other people would be most beneficial.

2. Introduce them to someone else

This may sound mean but if there is a business or life coach attending, what a perfect opportunity. There may be a great business or executive coach too that works well with people in their specific industry. If they are present at the event then make the introduction.

3.Ask permission

If you are feeling brave or you know that they are particularly hurting their reputations at this event, then ask permission to call them on their behavior. Be genuine and sincere in what you are trying to offer as advice in a logical non-confrontational manner. Empower them to come up with alternative options. 'Do you mind if I speak frankly with you?' and 'May I make a suggestion as to something that might increase your business currently'? 'Are you open to a suggestion'? Being diplomatic and with integrity may make all the difference, they may have been called on their actions before or they may be genuinely willing to learn, either way always ask politely for permission before diving in like a *Bird Of Prey* yourself.

Remember, we all have those *Bird Of Prey* moments, but by keeping ourselves present and true to others and the long term goals of our business in mind, then those moments will be short lived and noticed by oneself very quickly, your apologies can be made when necessary and integrity maintained. Build strong long lasting relationships, venture out and enjoy the sunshine.

About The Author

Author, speaker, coach, impresario, world-traveler, and Reality Networker: these are just a few words that describe the life that Tim Houston has led, (so far).

Tim owned and operated three successful businesses by the time he was 25. For more than a decade, he has dedicated himself to helping businesses of all sizes to become more productive, profitable and prosperous through referral-based marketing and business and social networking.

As a speaker, impresario and coach, Tim has positively impacted thousands of business people through his high-energy workshops, motivational presentations, and mentoring sessions on strategic business networking, public speaking, and word-of-mouth marketing strategies.

As an author, his work appeared in The New York Times Best Seller and multiple #1 Best Seller, *Masters of Sales*. His articles on the topic of business networking and word-of-mouth marketing have been translated and published in magazines, newspapers and blogs around the world. Over the years, Tim has been interviewed on many local TV and radio shows and has been featured in many articles including ***The New York Times, The New York Post, and New York Daily News.***

Tim loves to travel and has been to 20 countries and 35 US States. He's also an amateur magician, has two dogs, a cat, a bird and a fish. His secret to success is his commitment to help others become more productive, profitable, and prosperous in their businesses and their lives.

Visit www.worldsworstnetworker.com and www.tmhouston.com to keep up-to-date about Tim's books, programs and seminars. Contact Tim at tim@tmhouston.com; Twitter: @tmhouston Facebook: www.facebook.com/tmhouston

Contributors

Beth M. Anderson is an entrepreneur and an internationally recognized expert in word-of-mouth referral networking. She credits her success to the lessons learned by her participation in the world's largest organization of weekly face-to-face meetings, BNI.

She is the co-creator (along with **LuAnn Buechler)** of the internationally acclaimed, annual networking and educational event, "Get Connected!"

A website designer and developer by trade, she has her fingers in a number of different things at all times. Always passionate about the latest adventure, she loves learning new things, meeting new people, and tackling new challenges. Beth is the co-founder of OrgTrack.com and TheNetworkingClub.com. **Contact:** me@bethmanderson.com

Elaine Betts is the owner of Go Far Consulting, a management consulting firm. She was born in England and has lived in California since 1996. She has a formal education in microbiology and subsequent pharmaceutical research. Elaine also became a successful group director for a financial services company and realized that with goals and systems in place, anything can be achieved. With a Master Certificate in Applied Project Management, Elaine excels at working with attorneys, sales executives and team leaders.

Through her business endeavors her mission is to inspire and empower others to maximize their productivity and improve the working quality of their lives. Elaine is also known for her business networking abilities she is always looking for better ways to improve business relations. Her award and honors include: Contributing author to the New York Times and Multiple #1 Best-Seller, *Masters of Sales*, The Official Poet Laureate for the City of San Ramon, California and of BNI; formal recognition from Congress Woman Ellen Tauscher for joint commitment to business and the community and Elaine was also responsible for getting California Assembly Resolution #323 passed recognizing the first week of February as International Networking Week in California. **Contact:** Phone: 510-326-0763. Email: Elaine@gofarconsulting.com. Web: www.gofarconsulting.com

LuAnn Buechler is the co-creator (along with **Beth M. Anderson)** of the internationally acclaimed, annual networking and educational event, "Get Connected!" She is passionate about everything she does. LuAnn uses her unique personality and experiences to relate to the audience in delivering passionate presentations that inspire people to achieve the success they desire in business and in life. As a Certified Facilitator of *The Passion Test*, LuAnn shares with audiences a simply yet powerful system (Saving Yourself Time Energy & Money) to determine your true passions and set a course to living your life's destiny. As a director for BNI, LuAnn has built a repertoire of presentations on networking skills and relationship marketing which she uniquely relates to delivering high quality customer service. Caring is the ultimate competitive advantage. LuAnn delivers Customer Service training with the same passion that she delivers customer service in her own event management business. LuAnn has unique ability to capture the audience with her passionate, energetic personality. **Contact:** LuAnn Buechler, CMP , Professional Meeting Consultant, 512 Meadowlark Court Byron, MN 55920. E-mail: LuAnn@PMCEvents.com. Phone: 507-951-1468

Bob Burg shares information on topics vital to the success of today's business person. He speaks for corporations and associations internationally, including fortune 500 companies, franchises, and numerous direct sales organizations.
Sharing the principles contained in his bestselling books, Bob has addressed audiences ranging in size from 50 to 16,000, sharing the platform with notables including today's top thought leaders, broadcast personalities athletes and political leaders including cabinet secretaries and a former United States President.

His critically acclaimed book, *Endless Referrals: Network Your Everyday Contacts Into Sales* has sold over 200,000 copies and continues to be used as a training manual for top sales organizations throughout the world. His national bestseller, *The Go-Giver* has been heralded as a new business classic. It's been translated into 18 languages and is his fourth book to top the 150,000 copies sold mark.

He and his coauthor, John David Mann recently released their newest book, *Go-Givers Sell More*, which takes the Five Laws contained in their previous book and relates them specifically to the selling process.

Bob is an advocate, supporter and defender of the free enterprise system and seeks to empower individuals and organizations to thrive and grow by putting its principles to work.

He also puts his networking and go-giver abilities to use for charities, being a former Palm Beach County/Brooks Brothers Leukemia Society Man of the Year for his fundraising efforts on their behalf. A lover of animals, he is a former member of the Board of Directors of Safe Harbor, which is the Humane Society of Jupiter, Florida. **Contact:** Email: Bob@burg.com . Phone: 561 575-2114. Web: www.burg.com

Caroline Ceniza-Levine is a career coach, writer, speaker, multi-generational workplace expert and co-founder of SixFigureStart®, has 16 years of experience in professional services as a management consultant and executive and corporate recruiter. She has recruited for leading companies in media, financial services, management consulting, pharmaceuticals and technology. Caroline is a career columnist for CNBC.com, Vault.com, Wetfeet.com, and Forbes.com and an adjunct assistant professor of Professional Development at Columbia University School of International and Public Affairs. Caroline is a co-author (along with Donald Trump, Jack Canfield and others) of the best-selling *How the Fierce Handle Fear: Secrets to Succeeding in Challenging Times* (2010, Two Harbors Press). Her career advice and job market insights have been extensively quoted including mentions in NBC News.com, CBS Moneywatch, BusinessWeek, CareerBuilder, Christian Science Monitor, Newsweek, Real Simple, NPR and The Associated Press. Caroline is also a life coach (www.thinkasinc.com) and is a 2010 grant recipient of the Jones New York Empowerment Fund. Caroline is a graduate of Barnard College, Columbia University. **Contact:** Phone: 212-501-2234. Email: caroline@sixfigurestart.com. Web: www.sixfigurestart.com.

Jason Cobine runs a networking results company in the UK called 'Beyond Networking' where he teaches master classes on the introduction strategies that help professionals make the most of precious time, effort and resources. After Jason's classes, they find being introduced to the right people rewarding, easy, fun and profitable. Beyond Networking helps solicitors, accountants and selected other business with sales targets. They do that by helping their clients make the most out of the time and effort spent networking. They conduct one-on-one consultations as well as workshops to show their clients how to find profitable leads quickly and easily, online and offline. Jason also writes a popular blog, at www.beyondnetworking.co.uk/blog. **Contact**. Phone: 011 44 207 100 2457. Twitter: @JasonCobine.

Michelle R. Donovan is an International Best Selling Author and is known as "The Referability Expert" in Pittsburgh. She owns and operates Referral Institute of Western Pennsylvania. Michelle works with business owners who want to get more business by referral.

She has a Masters in Adult Education and is a Certified Instructor of Trainers. She has been a guest faculty for Penn State Beaver campus and the University of Pittsburgh's Katz Center for Executive Education.

As a writer, Michelle is a contributing author to multiple editions of the Training and Development Sourcebook. She writes a weekly blog (**www.thereferabilityexpert.blogspot.com**) that relates life to referral marketing. She has also published over 35 articles on networking and referral marketing in multiple publications. Michelle's first book, *The 29% Solution: 52 Weekly Networking Success Strategies*, co-authored with Dr. Ivan Misner, has been recognized as one of the top 30 business books of 2009 by Soundview Executive Book Summaries and hit #3 on the *Wall Street Journal* Best Sellers List.

As a speaker, Michelle has presented at several national and local conferences. She is known for combining meaningful substance through real-life application to learning. The key to her success is a supportive partner and surrounding herself with exceptional people.

Michelle is an avid cyclist, raising money for Multiple Sclerosis and Diabetes. When she's not on her bicycle, she's making homemade wine, riding her motorcycle, fishing on a lake or watching the her Pittsburgh Steelers

Contact: michelle@referralinstitutepittsburg.com. Web www.michellerdonovan.com. Phone: 724-816-1760

Robyn Henderson is a Global Networking Specialist. She has authored and contributed to over 25 books (including 10 on networking including the New York Time's #1 Best Seller, *Masters of Networking,* and business building and 3 on self-esteem and confidence building). Robyn has spoken in 12 countries and has never advertised. All of her work comes from networking, referrals and her website, www.networkingtowin.com.au

Her career includes over 20 years as a professional speaker, 10 years in sales and telemarketing management and 13 years in hospitality. Robyn also successfully ran women's networks for 6 years and was listed in the Businesswomen's Hall of Fame (1997) and listed in the Top 100 Spirited Women of Australia (New Woman Magazine).

Robyn was presented with the 1997 Speaker award from the National Speakers Association of Australia in November 1997 for her contribution to the speaking industry and is a CSP – Certified Speaking Professional with NSAA. This accreditation is shared by only 17 women in Australia and 110 women globally.

In 2000, Robyn received the prestigious Nevin Award – given annually to a member of NSAA whose accomplishments reflect outstanding credit, respect, honor and admiration of the entire speaking profession.

In 2003, Robyn was honored to be appointed Adjunct Professor at the Southern Cross University in Lismore, NSW, Australia. In 2004, Robyn successfully launched her latest venture Sea Change Publishing; Robyn held the position of Executive Officer with the National Speakers Association of Australia from 2007-2009.

Contact: Networking To Win, PO Box 1596, Kingscliff NSW 2487, Australia. Tel: 011 61 07 5523 0123
Fax: 011 61 07 5523 0153 Web: www.robynhenderson.com.
E-mail: robyn@networkingtowin.com.au

Sue Henry is known as the Workshop and Training Diva. She teaches and trains business owners how to increase profitability by actively seeking and receiving referrals. I write and deliver workshops, seminars, and teleconferences that provide practical, proven strategies in a systematic, do-able approach. She also write articles on referral and networking related topics that have been published on several online sites including SuccessNet, NetworkingNow, and The Networking Club. She is a contributing author to the *New York Times* and multiple #1 best-seller, "Masters of Sales". Sue's seminars that do more than educate and inspire, they deliver results and profits! **Contact**:
Phone: 507-269-1051 sue@suehenrytalks.com.
Web: www.suehenrytalks.com

Weston Lyon is the author of 14 books and a passionate professional speaker. Weston's entrepreneurial path has been a long one for only being 30 years young. He started his first business at age 20; and has since been involved in multiple businesses, ranging from skin care, to janitorial services, to gift incentive sales, to fitness coaching, to marketing and publishing. Today, Weston continues to have his hands in multiple businesses with the majority of his time spent writing and speaking to coaches and solo-entrepreneurs; as well as college students, when he gets the opportunity.

Weston lives in Sewickley; a small town outside Pittsburgh, PA. When he's not working, he's either on the playground with his son, Haven; or he's having fun practicing mixed marital arts, yoga, rock climbing, rollerblading, or any other adventurous, athletic activity he has the chance to do. You can pick up Weston's new book, <u>Overnight Success,</u> for FREE at www.WestonLyon.com. **Contact:** Phone: 412-974-0739. Email: westonlyon@westonlyon.com Web: www.WestonLyon.com.

Ivan R. Misner, Ph.D. is the Founder & Chairman of BNI, the world's largest business networking organization. BNI was founded in 1985. The organization has tens of thousands of members in thousands of chapters throughout every populated continent of the world. Each year, BNI members generate millions of business referrals resulting in billion of dollars worth of new business.

Dr. Misner's Ph.D. is from the University of Southern California. He is a *New York Times* Bestselling author who has written twelve books including his latest #1 bestseller *Networking Like a Pro.*

He is a monthly columnist for Entrepreneur.com and is the Senior Partner for the Referral Institute - a referral training company with trainers around the world. In addition, he has taught business management and social capital courses at several universities throughout the United States.

Called the *"Father of Modern Networking"* by CNN and the *"Networking Guru"* by Entrepreneur magazine, Dr. Misner is considered one of the world's leading experts on business networking and has been a keynote speaker for major corporations and associations throughout the world. He has been featured in the *L.A. Times, Wall Street Journal, and New York Times*, as well as numerous TV and radio shows including *CNN, CNBC,* and the *BBC* in London.

Dr. Misner is on the Board of Trustees for the University of La Verne. He is also the Founder of the BNI-Misner Foundation and was recently named "Humanitarian of the Year" by a Southern California newspaper. He is married and lives with his wife Elisabeth and their three children in Claremont, CA. **In his spare time!!!** he is also an amateur magician and a black belt in karate. **Contact:** Email: misner@bni.com. Phone: 1-800-825-8286. Web: www.bni.com. Blog: www.networkingentrepreneur.com

Mike Morrison is the owner of Mimo, a full service design, web and marketing agency in Newcastle Upon Tyne, UK who likes to do things a little differently. Mimo strives to provide a "be all and end all" solution for the needs of small-medium sized businesses looking to stand out for all of the right reasons. Whether that involves eye-catching graphic design, a stunning online presence, or a savvy approach to marketing their business; Mimo strive to deliver above and beyond every time. Mike's blog is www.mimomedia.co.uk/blog/ and his YouTube channel is www.youtube.com/user/ThisIsMimo. **Contact:** Phone: 011 44 0845 900 5771. Email: hello@mimomedia.co.uk Web: www.mimomedia.co.uk

Susan RoAne leads a double life as a bestselling author and a sought-after *professional keynote speaker*. Known as The Mingling Maven®, she gives diverse audiences the required tools, techniques and strategies they need to connect and communicate in today's global business world. Her practical, informative, and interactive presentations are known for what *The San Francisco Chronicle* calls her "dynamite sense of humor." RoAne's audiences learn how to work a room and master the art of face to face communication in any setting. With her timeless tips, anyone can overcome shyness and learn to schmooze with confidence in business networking or social gatherings. As a professional keynote speaker, some of the organizations that have hired Susan are: AT&T, Apple, Coca-Cola, Time Warner, Office Depot, Boeing, Citigroup, Ernst and Young, United States Department of The Treasury, Oracle, Procter and Gamble, United States Air Force, National Football League and, her personal favorite, Hershey's Chocolate.

Because of her groundbreaking best-seller, *How to Work a Room®,* Susan RoAne is considered one of the most influential networking and business communication experts. She has sold over a million books worldwide, and helped launch an industry that she continues to recreate and shape today.

Susan RoAne received her Master's Degree from San Francisco State University and her Bachelor's from the University of Illinois Champaign-Urbana, where she was honored at "Authors Come Home". (She still considers herself a Fighting Ilini!) A former teacher, Susan is also a sought-after college keynote speaker at major universities such as Yale, Wharton, University of Chicago and NYU.

A resident of the beautiful San Francisco Bay Area, Susan is a member of The National Speakers Association, The Authors Guild, the MS society, a Supporter of The Mill Valley Film Festival, as well as a Friend of the San Francisco Ballet. **Contact:** Email: susan@susanroane.com. Web: www.susanroane.com

Tara Schmakel a/k/a *The Once Timid Networker,* is the owner of the Workroom at Tara's, was born and raised in Alaska. She has been sewing since a little girl with her Mother and Grandmother. After doing various needle arts for business and pleasure, she settled on sewing for the home creating the Workroom at Tara's. Her work has been displayed in ASID showcase homes, on HGTV and published in Better Homes and Gardens magazines and books, Midwest Home and Mpls./St. Paul Magazine. Tara is also the Executive Chair of The Entrepreneural Excellence

Business Forums in Minneapolis where she assists entrepreneurs to run their businesses effectively and efficiantly through knowledge, relationships and support. **Contact**: Phone: 952.240.3834. Email: tara@myworkroom.com. Blog: thetimidnetworkrer.blogspot.com.

Bijay Shah is the National Director for BNI United Arab Emirates, and has recently taken up the challenge to be the National Director for BNI Kenya. In addition to this, Bijay is a franchise partner for The Referral Institute – the ultimate word-of-mouth sales program in Dubai. A qualified Financial Advisor by profession, with more than 10 years of experience in the financial services industry, Bijay has helped numerous clients on 3 Continents - Africa, Europe & Middle East - in building and protecting their wealth. Achieving personal excellence and helping members realize their fullest potential are the fuel for Bijay's limitless energy. Bijay's burning desires are to create a community of business people that believes in building business through trust and cooperative efforts i.e. "Givers Gain" and to make BNI membership synonymous with business growth! Always warm, friendly, caring and approachable, Bijay is a Coach and Mentor for many on their life's Journey to Success. **Contact:** Email: bijay@bni-me.com

Kevin Snow is a sales and marketing professional from the Twin Cities, Minnesota with over 15 years experience as a sales leader in the technology and internet marketing industries. He is an author and a professional speaker specializing in word of mouth marketing and how to best tell your story to get business. Currently Kevin is serving as an Area Director with BNI Minnesota and has over 1100 members in his area that closed over $25,000,000 of business during 2010 just through referrals.

Kevin is the owner of Time On Target, a professional public speaking and corporate training firm specializing in helping companies hit their business targets through better communication and more effective networking. He is also a partner in Norton Creative Group, a successful web design company. Kevin is an officer in the US Army and brings a unique look at relationship building across cultures to help you build your business in our ever shrinking world.

Through his interactive workshops, Kevin helps participants learn skills and techniques they can immediately implement within their businesses that impact the quality and effectiveness of the message they are presenting to their audiences and most importantly build bigger and better networks. **Contact:** Email: kevin@bni-mn.com. Blog: kevinsnow.wordpress.com

Jan Vermeiren is the founder of Networking Coach and according to HR Tribune one of Belgiums top 10 speakers. Jan and his team not only provide (key note) presentations, training courses and personal coaching about networking and referrals, but also advice organizations how to stimulate networking at their own events and how to integrate networking in their sales and recruitment strategy. He is regularly interviewed as an expert about online and offline networking, LinkedIn and referrals by different media like Belgian national television (De Zevende Dag, Lichtpunt), Forbes, several newspapers, job sites (Vacature.com, Jobat) and the magazines of several Chambers of Commerce.

Jan is the author of the networking book 'Let's Connect!', the networking CD 'Let's Connect at an event!', the 'Everlasting Referrals Home Study Course' and this book 'How to REALLY use LinkedIn'.

The US version of 'Let's Connect!' reached the Amazon best seller list on October 9, 2007 with a number 2 position in marketing books and number 9 in management books. This made Jan the first Belgian author to reach this position.

On March 17, 2009 he broke his own record on Amazon when "How to REALLY use LinkedIn" reached number 1 position in the category "Sales and Selling" and number 2 position in the category "Job Hunting and Careers".

Jan and his team are hired as speaker and trainer by large international companies like Alcatel, Deloitte, DuPont, IBM,

ING, Mobistar, Nike, SAP and Sun Microsystems as well as by small companies and freelancers.

Jan is also a speaker and guest lecturer in the international MBA programs of Vlerick Leuven Gent Management School (Belgium) and RSM Erasmus University Rotterdam (the Netherlands). As a networking and LinkedIn expert, he teaches these students how to get a job by tapping into the power of their network.

Due to the success of the book "How to REALLY use LinkedIn" Jan and his team came in contact with LinkedIn's management team. This resulted in the certification of Networking Coach as the first LinkedIn Certified Training Partner in the world.

Contact: Email: connect-with-us@networking-coach.com. Blog: www.janvermeiren.com. Web: www.networking-coach.com

Jerry W. Williamson is the CEO of Teamworx Productions, a company which helps business owners, managers and executives understand the importance of excelling in team building in order to exponentially grow their company from the ground up.

Jerry is also an Area Director for BNI of North Alabama, who has won Director Performance Evaluation Awards for outstanding leadership evaluations at BNI National Conferences in 2008 and 2009. He was also named Ambassador of the Year for the Huntsville Madison County Chamber of Commerce in 2008 and is called the "Ambassador of Networking" throughout North Alabama. With a B.S. degree in Communications, he enjoys writing his blogs on www.jerrywwilliamson.com and is a contributing writer to BNI's SuccessNet newsletter, Ezine.com, and Examiner.com.

Jerry believes that in order for people to retain what they learn they must be involved in the process, so his teaching style has been developed to be very interactive, creative and a lot of fun. Jerry is known for empowering his audience for results. **Contact:** Phone: (256) 679-6227. Web: www.teamworxproductions.com

Tony Wolfe is a voice actor, MC, speaker/presenter, writer and has been heard around the globe. With his motivating GO DO!™ attitude, he will surely bring a positive and productive result to any project or event. Known as "The Man Of A Thousand Voices," he began his voice acting career performing characters and impersonations for a morning drive-time radio show in 1985. This afforded him fourteen well-invested years of experience where he developed characters, wrote and performed in comedy bits and provided voiceovers for commercials and imaging projects. He even made comedy stage appearances as some of the characters he portrayed on the show.

Some of Tony's projects include: an animated children's program where he provided voices for eight of the fifteen characters in the pilot. He is the voice of Fischers Meats' "Mr. Bologna" and his Jimmy Stewart impersonation has been used as a promo for NBC's TODAY Show. He is also the voice of The Redneck Horn, which was featured on The Tonight Show with Jay Leno as one of the best novelty Christmas gifts of 2004 which later became the second best selling novelty item in Spencer Gifts stores nationwide.

Tony also provides more serious reads for a wide variety of projects. For example, he has been in the emergency services arena since 1986 as a firefighter/medic and a medicolegal death investigator where his voice adds a level of knowledge and sincerity for projects in the medical and law enforcement related fields Tony is listed in several talent pools and his voice is used for projects in numerous studios all over the United States, Canada and Australia. Whether it is on hold messages, online college courses, training videos, podcasts, audio books or characters for any application Tony is always eagerly seeking new opportunities to expand and diversify his talent portfolio.

He is also is an Area Director for BNI in Tennese, Kentucky and Southern Indiana.   **Contact**: Email: tw@tonywolfe.com   Web: www.tonywolfe.com

Printed in Great Britain
by Amazon.co.uk, Ltd.,
Marston Gate.